RECOLLECTIONS OF A
PENINSULAR VETERAN

Lt. Col. Joseph Anderson, C.B.

LONDON EDWARD ARNOLD.

RECOLLECTIONS OF A PENINSULAR VETERAN

BY THE LATE

LT.-COLONEL JOSEPH ANDERSON
C.B., KNIGHT OF HANOVER
OF THE 78TH, 24TH, AND 50TH REGIMENTS
(1805—1848)

The Naval & Military Press Ltd

Reproduced by kind permission of the Central Library,
Royal Military Academy, Sandhurst

Published by
The Naval & Military Press Ltd
Unit 10, Ridgewood Industrial Park,
Uckfield, East Sussex,
TN22 5QE England
Tel: +44 (0) 1825 749494
Fax: +44 (0) 1825 765701
www.naval-military-press.com
www.military-genealogy.com

© The Naval & Military Press Ltd 2010

The Naval & Military Press ...

...offer specialist books for the serious student of conflict. The range of titles stocked covers the whole spectrum of military history with titles on uniforms, battles, official histories, specialist works containing Medal Rolls and Casualties Lists, and numismatic titles for medal collectors and researchers.

The innovative approach they have to military bookselling and their commitment to publishing have made them Britain's leading independent military bookseller.

In reprinting in facsimile from the original, any imperfections are inevitably reproduced and the quality may fall short of modern type and cartographic standards.

INTRODUCTION

THE following pages have been selected from the autobiography of my grandfather, the late Colonel Joseph Anderson, who was born in Sutherlandshire, Scotland, on June 1, 1790, and died on July 18, 1877. It should be stated that this narrative was written only for his own family. He had never kept a diary—nor even any notes of his adventures and travels—and only began to write his reminiscences of the long-past years when he was seventy-four, in the quiet of his beautiful home near Melbourne, Australia. His memory was perfectly amazing; but if any slight inaccuracies should be discovered, the reader is asked to excuse them, on account of his age. He was a "grand old man" in every sense, and lived in excellent health of mind and body until his eighty-eighth year. To the very last he was always keenly interested in military matters, and never failed to attend, in uniform, all the important volunteer reviews held in Melbourne, where his upright, soldierly figure attracted universal admiration. His son, the late Colonel

Acland Anderson, C.M.G., was for many years the Colonel-Commandant of the Military Forces of H.M. Government in Victoria, which appointment he held till his death in January, 1882. He was the founder of the Volunteer Organization, as in 1855 he raised a Rifle Corps in Melbourne, which was not only the first in Victoria but probably the first in Australia.

ACLAND ANDERSON,
Captain, late 3rd Dragoon Guards.

SEPTEMBER, 1913.

CONTENTS

CHAPTER I
EARLY EXPERIENCES 1

Born in Scotland—At fifteen years old appointed to the 78th Regiment—First visit to London—Join regiment at Shorncliffe—Embark for Gibraltar—Put under arrest—Lieutenant James Mackay

CHAPTER II
THE CAMPAIGN OF MAIDA 10

Expedition to Calabria—In General Acland's brigade—Battle of Maida—Sergeant McCrae and the wounded Frenchman—Reggio—Capture of Catrone—Taormina—Syracuse

CHAPTER III
IN EGYPT 17

Expedition to Egypt—We take possession of Alexandria—Entrapped by the enemy at Rosetta—A trying retreat

CHAPTER IV
THE EL-HAMET DISASTER 23

Colonel McLeod's death and losses of his detachment—Captain Mackay honoured by Turkish Pasha—Return to Sicily—78th goes to England—Attack of ophthalmia

CHAPTER V

THE BATTLE OF TALAVERA 30

Gazetted to lieutenancy in 24th Regiment—Embarked for Portugal—Battle of Talavera—Wounded—Soldiers seize Spanish pigs

CHAPTER VI

THE BATTLE OF BUSACO 38

Army kindly received in Portugal—Much fighting with French army under Massena—Lord Wellington's retreat on the Lines of Torres Vedras—Battle of Busaco

CHAPTER VII

THE LINES OF TORRES VEDRAS 47

Continued fighting—General Beresford knighted—English and French officers spend evenings together at theatres, etc., with consent of their commanders—Massena retires to Santarem

CHAPTER VIII

THE LOST REGIMENTAL BOOKS 54

Story of the lost regimental books and the honesty of the soldiers

CHAPTER IX

THE BATTLE OF FUENTES D'ONORO . . . 61

Much fighting—We drive the enemy across the Mondego at Coimbra—Battle of Fuentes d'Onoro—I go into the French lines to take away the body of a friend

CONTENTS

CHAPTER X

IN SCOTLAND 70

On sick-leave in England—In Scotland—Journey of seventy miles in twenty-four hours on foot after a ball—Appointed to assist at brigade office, 1813—Appointed captain and brigade major in the York Chasseurs

CHAPTER XI

VOYAGE TO BARBADOS 76

Portsmouth—Guernsey—Sail for Barbados—Honest Henry—Frightful storm—Adventure at Funchal

CHAPTER XII

ST. VINCENT AND GUADELOUPE 87

Life in Barbados—I am appointed acting-paymaster—President of a court-martial—Deputy judge-advocate—At St. Vincent—Expedition to Guadeloupe—Appointed deputy assistant quartermaster-general and sent to Guadeloupe

CHAPTER XIII

DOMINICA 96

Sent to Dominica—A fatal foot-race—I give up appointment and rejoin my regiment at St. Vincent—An awful voyage

CHAPTER XIV

AN AMUSING DUEL 103

Jamaica — Return to England — York Chasseurs disbanded—Trip to France—An amusing duel

CHAPTER XV

CHASED BY A PIRATE 112

Appointed captain in the 50th Regiment—Embark for Jamaica—A terrible storm and a drunken captain—Return to port—Sail again with another captain—Ship chased by a pirate—Jamaica once more

CHAPTER XVI

LIFE IN JAMAICA 123

Appointed deputy judge-advocate—Sir John Keane—An interesting court-martial—Sent with a small detachment to Port Maria—Awful outbreak of yellow fever

CHAPTER XVII

HOME AGAIN AND MARRIED 132

Invalided to England—Ship injured on coral rock—Dangerous voyage—Married on 25th November, 1826—Portsmouth—The Duke of Clarence—Ireland—Complimented by Sir Hussey Vivian on execution of difficult manœuvres

CHAPTER XVIII

TO NEW SOUTH WALES 142

Dr. Doyle's sermon—Ordered to New South Wales—Sail for Sydney with three hundred convicts—Mutiny at Norfolk Island—Appointed colonel-commandant there

CHAPTER XIX

NORFOLK ISLAND 151

Life at Norfolk Island—Trial of the mutineers—A fresh conspiracy—Execution of thirteen mutineers

CONTENTS xi

CHAPTER XX

PAGE
SUNDAY SERVICES AT NORFOLK ISLAND . . . 158

I appoint two convicts (who had been educated for the Church) to officiate—Find about a hundred ex-soldiers among the convicts—Separate them from the others, with great success

CHAPTER XXI

LIFE AT NORFOLK ISLAND 166

Solitary case of misconduct among the soldier gang—I get many pardoned and many sentences shortened—Theatricals and other amusements—Visit from my brother—Mr. MacLeod

CHAPTER XXII

MANGALORE CATTLE STATION 174

Wreck of the *Friendship*—I am attacked by Captain Harrison and MacLeod—I receive the Royal Guelphic Order of Knighthood—Secure the sheep and cattle station of "Mangalore" in Port Phillip with my brother—Leave Norfolk Island—Visit to Mangalore

CHAPTER XXIII

ON MY DEFENCE 186

Court of inquiry as to my management of Norfolk Island—Major Bunbury reprimanded by Commander-in-Chief at the Horse Guards for his unfounded charges

CHAPTER XXIV

ORDERED TO CALCUTTA 193

50th Regiment ordered to India—Sudden death of one of my boys—Voyage to India—First experiences of Calcutta

CHAPTER XXV

LIFE AT CALCUTTA 200

Magnificent entertainments at Calcutta — Dost Mahomet—Wreck of the *Ferguson*—Preparations for Burmese campaign—Special favour shown to soldiers of the 50th Regiment

CHAPTER XXVI

AT MOULMEIN 209

Great welcome to Moulmein—No fighting after all—The Madras native regiments

CHAPTER XXVII

VOYAGE UP THE GANGES 215

Return to Calcutta—Much illness in regiment—Boat journey of three months to Cawnpore—Incidents of the voyage—Death of Daniel Shean

CHAPTER XXVIII

IN COMMAND AT CAWNPORE 223

Life at Cawnpore—Quarrel between Mowatt and Burke—Court-martial

CHAPTER XXIX

THE GWALIOR CAMPAIGN 229

Expedition to Gwalior—In command of the regiment—Brigadier Black—His accident—I am appointed to the command of the brigade—Battle of Punniar—In General Gray's absence I order a charge on the enemy's guns—Severely wounded

CONTENTS xiii

CHAPTER XXX

WOUNDED AND MADE MUCH OF 240

"My brigade had carried all before it"—Painful return to camp—General Gray's dispatch

CHAPTER XXXI

RETURN TO CAWNPORE 247

Slow recovery from my wound—Painful journey by palanquin to Cawnpore—Am created a C.B.—Other honours and promotions

CHAPTER XXXII

ON LEAVE FOR TWO YEARS 253

Riding accident at Cawnpore—Foot seriously injured —Get two years' leave of absence—Voyage to Cape Town—On to Australia—A strange cabin

CHAPTER XXXIII

AUSTRALIA ONCE MORE 260

Sydney once more—Visit Mangalore—Select land for house near Melbourne—My War Medal

CHAPTER XXXIV

SECOND VOYAGE TO CALCUTTA 266

Sail for India—Dangers of Torres Straits—Copang —Arrival at Calcutta—My son appointed to the 50th Regiment

CHAPTER XXXV

To Cawnpore and Back 274

Violent gale at Loodhiana — Two hundred men, women, and children buried — By river steamer to Allahabad — Rejoin the regiment at Cawnpore — Return voyage down the Ganges

CHAPTER XXXVI

India to Cape Town 281

The guns captured in the Sutlej campaign—Lord Hardinge's compliments to the regiment—I secure compensation for the regiment's losses at Loodhiana—Voyage to Cape Town

CHAPTER XXXVII

Return to England 289

Return to England—Continued in command of the regiment

CHAPTER XXXVIII

Farewell to the 50th Regiment . . . 296

Decide to retire—Return to Australia

ORDERS AND MEDALS

OF THE LATE

LIEUT.-COLONEL JOSEPH ANDERSON, C.B., K.H.,

OF THE 50TH (QUEEN'S OWN) REGIMENT,

And of Fairlie House, South Yarra, near Melbourne, Victoria.

Born July 1st, 1790.   Died 18th July, 1877.

LIEUT.-COLONEL ANDERSON'S SERVICES.

"Expedition to Calabria, including the battle of Maida, and subsequent operations, and capture of the fortress of Catrone; expedition to Egypt in 1807; Peninsular War from April, 1809, to January, 1812, including the battles of Talavera (wounded) and Busaco; retreat to the Lines of Torres Vedras and various affairs there; with the advance at Espinhal, battle of Fuentes d'Onoro, and many other affairs and skirmishes. (War Medal with four clasps.) Served at the capture of Guadeloupe in 1815. Commanded a brigade at the battle of Punniar (medal), and was severely wounded at its head when in the act of charging the enemy's guns."—*Hart's Army List.*

1. "MILITARY ORDER OF THE BATH," founded by King George I, 25th May, 1725.

2. "THE GUELPHIC ORDER" (Hanoverian), founded by King George IV, when Prince Regent, in the name of his father, George III, on 12th August, 1815.

3. "THE WAR MEDAL," granted by the Queen, 1st June, 1847, for services in the Peninsular War (4 clasps) :—

    1. Maida, July 4, 1806.
    2. Talavera, July 27 and 28, 1809.
    3. Busaco, September 27, 1810.
    4. Fuentes d'Onoro, May 5, 1811.

    The War Medal has on the obverse the head of the Queen, with the date, 1848; and on the reverse Her Majesty, as the representative of the country or people, is in the act of crowning with a laurel wreath the Duke of Wellington, in a kneeling attitude, as emblematic of the army.

4. MAHRATTA CAMPAIGN OF 1843: "INDIAN STAR OF BRONZE," made from the captured guns. Battle of Punniar, 29th December, 1843.

    "About four o'clock in the afternoon the enemy was observed to have taken up a strong position on a chain of lofty hills four miles eastward of the camp. . . . The Second Infantry Brigade, under Brigadier Anderson, of the 50th, arrived in time to put a finish to the action; forming on the crest of a hill, he, by a gallant and judicious movement, attacked the enemy's left, and completely defeated him, taking the remainder of his guns. . . . Major White took the Second Infantry Brigade out of action upon Brigadier Anderson being wounded."—Carter's "Medals of the British Army."

RECOLLECTIONS OF A PENINSULAR VETERAN

CHAPTER I

EARLY EXPERIENCES

Born in Scotland—At fifteen years old appointed to the 78th Regiment—First visit to London—Join regiment at Shorncliffe—Embark for Gibraltar—Put under arrest—Lieutenant James Mackay

I SUDDENLY and most unexpectedly got my commission as an ensign in the 78th Regiment (27th June, 1805) through the influence of my brother William, a captain in the same corps, being then only within a few days of my fifteenth year. But before I go any further I must mention an amusing incident which took place before I left Banff Academy to join my regiment, and as in the present day it may not appear much to my credit, I beg my dear ones who may read this to remember I was still a boy, and with less experience of the world than most of the youths of the present day. Out of my pocket money I managed to save six shillings, with which I purchased an old gun to amuse myself, and to shoot sparrows during our play hours; and this being contrary to all rules and positive standing orders, I kept my dangerous weapon at an old woman's house a little way from town. A few chosen companions knew of my secret and accompanied me one evening to enjoy our sport, but there was one amongst them to whom I refused a shot, so next day he reported me and my gun to the second master. I was called up and questioned on his evidence, when I stoutly and boldly denied every word he said. The good master, Mr. Simpson, then said, "You have told a lie, sir, and I must punish you; so down with your breeches." I at once resisted, and said, "I am an officer and won't submit." He then called two or three boys to assist him in clearing for action, but I still resisted, and kicked and thumped them all round, until the noise became so loud that the good old rector came in from his room and said, "What is all this?" On his being told, and also my reasons for resisting, he laughed most heartily and said, "I will not disgrace you, sir; you are an officer, and I will not disgrace you." So I was allowed to escape and to go back to my seat. Many years afterwards I returned to Banff, and the rector and I had many laughs over this frolic, and at the same time I met Mr. Simpson, but found it difficult to convince him of my continued good will, and that I never forgot the good and salutary lesson he gave me.

Six weeks after this I received a letter from my brother ordering me to join my regiment, then stationed at Shorncliffe barracks in Kent, and directing me at the same time to go in the first instance to my uncle, Dr. Anderson, at Peterhead, to receive an outfit, and then, without being allowed to go home to see my father, I was shipped off for London in one of the trading sloops of that day, and consigned to another friend of ours, Mr. Tod, who was married to my only aunt. They received me most kindly, and here I found a number of young ladies, my cousins, who were about my own age, and with whom I soon became happy and intimate. I remained with them for a fortnight, and during that time Mr. Tod took me to his tailor, who furnished me with all my necessary regimentals, and not a little proud was I on finding myself for the first time dressed out in scarlet and gold. Mr. Tod took me also to many of the public places and streets of London, and to this day I cannot forget how the good old man laughed at my surprise and remarks about all the pretty women who unblushingly stared at me.

On the 18th August, 1805, I took my leave, and by coach proceeded to join my regiment at Shorncliffe barracks. My brother William received me on my arrival, and then took me to the colonel to introduce me, and afterwards to the adjutant to report my arrival, and then to my future home for a time, his own house at Sandgate; and with him I remained for two months, until we marched for Portsmouth to embark for Gibraltar. In the meantime I attended all daily parades, morning and evening, and was drilled and instructed in a squad with the men.

But before I go any further I must mention that soon after joining the regiment my brother told me I was never regularly gazetted to my ensigncy. That appointment had been given to my brother John, who at the same time got a cadetship in the Madras Army, which my father considered the best appointment of the two, and consequently wrote to my brother William to use his interest with General McKenzie Fraser, the full colonel of the 78th (from whom the ensigncy was procured), to say that his brother John was provided for, but that he had another brother, Joseph, to whom he hoped he would kindly transfer the commission; and this the general at once consented to do, and so I was ordered to join, and for nearly two years after my name appeared ". . . Anderson" in the Army List. Such chances do not happen nowadays.

We arrived at Portsmouth at the beginning of October, and embarked on the following day for Gibraltar. The transports of those days were wretched, and their provisions were even worse, and in the miserable tub *Neptune*, to which I was doomed, we were so crowded that I, as the youngest subaltern, had neither berth nor cot allowed me, and I was obliged to double up with another young ensign, and to make the best I could of it. Yet we were very jolly, and all went on well until we got off Lisbon, about the 19th of October, when the commodore of all the other ships-of-war in charge of the convoy made the signal, "An enemy in sight, put in to port in view," and this was immediately answered by every ship in the convoy. The whole fleet then went about and steered direct for Lisbon, and so we continued with every sail set, until on the same evening, and following day, we were all safely at anchor in the Tagus. We heard soon after, that the enemy we discovered in time was part of the French fleet then making for Trafalgar, and in a few days more we had the great and glorious news of Nelson's splendid and complete victory over the combined fleets of France and Spain off Cape Trafalgar, on the 21st October, 1805, and of their almost complete capture and destruction. But, alas! how great was the price of this national success, for Nelson fell, and many gallant officers, soldiers, and sailors with him.

A few days after receiving this great news we again sailed from Lisbon for Gibraltar, and beyond Cape Trafalgar we came up with our own partly dismasted and disabled ships, and all which could be safely brought away of the enemy's captured vessels, the former proudly distinguished by their English tattered flags, and the latter humbled by the British ensign flying triumphantly over the national emblems of France and Spain. This was indeed a proud sight, and a lasting day of triumph and renown to old England, for from that time to the present hour the might of the Spanish navy was crushed and the French navy never appeared formidable to us again. We soon passed our noble heroes and their prizes, and our fleet reached Gibraltar a few days afterwards.

The regiment landed next day, and occupied Windmill Hill and Europa Point barracks. There were no less than four other regiments there when we arrived, and I liked that gay station very much. But there for the first and only time of my military life I was put in arrest, and became so alarmed that I cried bitterly, and thought I was going to be hanged at least! The other ensigns of the regiment were all many years older than I, and one of them in particular used to bully and annoy me constantly, so that on one of these occasions I made use of most insulting and ungentlemanlike language to him. Our kind and parental colonel (Macleod of Guinnes) was then in the habit of inviting all the young officers to breakfast with him, and on the following morning I went as usual in full dress to his house, about a mile from our barracks, and there on entering I found Cameron seated with others. The colonel soon appeared, and wished all good morning in his accustomed kind manner and asked us to take our seats. Breakfast passed over as usual. As soon as the table was cleared Colonel Macleod stood up and called us all to him, and then, addressing me, said, " Mr. Anderson, Mr. Cameron has reported to me that you have been making use of most improper language to him, and as you seem to forget you are no longer a schoolboy, but an officer, I must put you under arrest, and send you home in disgrace to your family. Leave your sword there, sir [on the table], and go to your barracks immediately." Poor me! I at once showed I was still but a schoolboy, for I cried and sobbed fearfully, and returned to my barracks with a broken heart.

The same evening a dear friend of my family, Captain John Mackay of Bighouse, called on me (no doubt at the request of the colonel), and frightened me more than ever, for he told me again that I would be brought to a general court-martial and deprived of my commission. I now cried more than ever, and I told him all that had passed between me and Cameron, and the constant insults and liberties he attempted to take with me in the presence of the other officers. I was glad to see from my friend's remarks that he began to think Cameron was more to blame than I was, yet he still told me

I must prepare for the worst, and so he left me to my own misery. I shall never forget my sufferings that night. However, next day I was ordered to attend at the colonel's quarters, and there found most of the officers assembled, Cameron amongst them. The colonel then addressed us, and said, "Mr. Anderson, I have been inquiring into your conduct, and find that you, Mr. Cameron, most grossly insulted this young gentleman, and by your daring, unwarrantable, and most unofficerlike conduct provoked a young boy to forget himself. You, sir, are many years older and ought to know better; I consider you therefore far more culpable and blameable in every respect than Mr. Anderson. You have both acted very improperly, but for the present I shall take no further notice of your conduct than with this reprimand to warn you both to be more careful and correct for the future; and now, Mr. Anderson, you are released from your arrest, and will return to your duty." Off I went in joy to my barracks, thankful indeed for this proper support and friendly admonition, and from that day I enjoyed myself and felt happy with my brother officers.

I was at this time attached to a company commanded by an old and experienced officer, Lieutenant James Mackay, a most studious man, and an acknowledged scholar, whose pride, next to his profession, was in his books. His instruction and care did me more good than any previous or subsequent opportunities I ever had for study. I was quartered with him at Europa Point, and he made me rise early and visit our men's barracks at Windmill Hill, two miles distant, every morning. I then returned to breakfast with him, after which we went to our public parade, which was no sooner over than we got home, and then he made me sit down to certain books and studies which he gave me. This he made me continue daily while we remained at Gibraltar, although (at the instigation of the other officers) I often tricked him, and tried hard to get off from such control and (as I then thought) drudgery. Being a perfect master of the French language, he was one of the British officers sent with Napoleon Bonaparte to the island of St. Helena, and afterwards recalled by our Government on the suspicion of being too intimate with the ex-Emperor.

CHAPTER II

THE CAMPAIGN OF MAIDA

Expedition to Calabria—In General Acland's brigade—Battle of Maida—Sergeant McCrae and the wounded Frenchman—Reggio—Capture of Catrone—Taormina—Syracuse

EARLY in 1806 our regiment left Gibraltar for Messina, where we continued some months, and then marched for Milazzo, where we camped until we embarked, in June of the same year, as a part of the expedition under Lieut.-General Sir John Stuart for Calabria, landing with the other troops in the gulf of St. Euphemia on the morning of the 1st of July. The object of this force was to attack the French General Regnier, then in that part of Italy with a considerable army. Our landing was but slightly opposed, because our convoy, the *Endymion* frigate (Captain Hoste), took up her position as near the shore as possible, and by her fire soon cleared the beach and drove the enemy far beyond our first footing. He made a partial stand, however, on a rising ground

THE CAMPAIGN OF MAIDA 11

inland; but as our troops advanced, and after a skirmish, we soon forced him to retreat on his supports and finally on his main body. We then halted for the day, and the enemy left advanced posts and videttes to watch our movements. We soon bivouacked for the night about 6 miles from the beach, with, of course, the same precautions. During that evening and the following day we were busily engaged in landing our heavy stores of provisions. On the 3rd July we advanced a few miles to reconnoitre and to gain information of the enemy's force and main position, and on the memorable and beautiful morning of the 4th July we finally advanced in columns, and soon found ourselves on the unusually clear and extensive plain of Maida, the enemy showing in mass on the distant hills and woods, about three miles from us, with a river in front which greatly strengthened their position.

As soon as we got half across the plain, our columns were halted, and the troops deployed into two lines, the one to support the other, with our skirmishers thrown out in front to cover us. We were then directed to "order arms and stand at ease"; thus formed, we offered a fair field to the enemy. Our brigade, consisting of the 58th, 78th, and 81st Regiments, under General Acland, formed our front line, and in this position we remained at least half an hour gazing at our enemy; by this time the French were seen in full view debouching from the hills and woods, and, crossing the river, they advanced with all confidence towards us. As soon as they had cleared the river their advance halted, and the whole then formed into two columns, in which order they steadily advanced with drums playing and colours flying. We remained quiet and steady, but impatient, on our ground, and had a full view of our foes, as they boldly and confidently advanced, evidently expecting that they could, and would, walk over us; and so they ought to have done, for we afterwards ascertained they numbered upwards of nine thousand of their best troops, while our force did not much exceed six thousand men! Their cavalry was also more numerous, for we had only one squadron of the 23rd Light Dragoons; but ours was so admirably managed that it kept the others in check during the whole day.

As soon as these formidable French columns came sufficiently near, and not till then, our lines were called to "attention" and ordered to "shoulder arms." Then commenced in earnest the glorious battle of Maida, first with a volley from our brigade into the enemy's columns and from our artillery at each flank without ceasing, followed by independent file firing as fast as our men could load; and well they did their work! Nor were the enemy idle; they returned our fire without ceasing, then in part commenced to deploy into line. The independent file firing was still continued with more vigour than ever for at least a quarter of an hour, when many brave men fell on both sides. Our brigade was then ordered to charge, supported by our second line, and this they did lustily and with endless hearty cheers, the French at the same moment following our example and advancing towards us at a steady charge of bayonets, the rolling of drums, and endless loud cheers. Both armies were equally determined to carry all before them; it was not till we got within five or six paces of each other that the enemy wavered, broke their ranks, and gave way, turning away to a man and scampering off, most of them throwing away their arms at the same time; but our men continued their cheers and got up with some of them, and numbers were either bayoneted, shot, or taken prisoners. The enemy was then fairly driven over the bridge by which they had advanced, or forced into the river, where numbers were captured or drowned.

Our loss was comparatively small. The brave 78th had about a dozen men killed and many wounded. The 20th Regiment landed during the action, and by an able and hurried manœuvre managed to get on the enemy's right flank, and contributed much to the success of the day. Captain McLean, of that regiment, was the only officer killed in the battle. I shall never forget my horror when I beheld numbers of gallant French soldiers weltering in their blood and groaning in agony from the most fearful wounds. And here I must mention an incident to the honour and credit of one of our Highland sergeants of grenadiers, Farquhar McCrae, who could not speak one word of English nor of French. He was wounded after we had passed over the first line of dead and dying Frenchmen, and while passing through the heap of wounded one of them made him a sign that he wanted a drink, on which McCrae immediately turned round and made towards the river; but he had no sooner done so, than his ungrateful enemy levelled his musket and wounded him slightly in the arm. McCrae looked back, saw from whom the shot came, and going up to the man he seized his firelock, and after a struggle soon got it away from him; then, taking it by the muzzle, raised the butt over the Frenchman's head and said, with a terrible Gaelic oath, "I'll knock your brains out!" But a more generous impulse seized him; he actually went back to the river and brought the wretched man some water!

I have heard that in Lieut.-General Sir John Stewart's official dispatch concerning the battle of Maida it is stated that the bayonets of the contending forces actually crossed during the charge. They may have done so, in some parts of the line—but *so far as I could see* they did not do so, and I have never heard any one who was in the action say that "the bayonets actually crossed."

The defeat was perfect, and the victory glorious beyond all praise. We remained on the field of battle burying our dead and attending the wounded and embarking our prisoners; then we marched for Reggio, the castle of which was then besieged by some others of our troops from Sicily, who now joined our force, except the 78th Regiment, which was at once embarked under convoy of the *Endymion* frigate and destined for the capture of the fortress of Catrone, on the east coast of Italy. We arrived and anchored off that place. About a week afterwards the *Endymion* took up her position within range of the fort, and all were ordered to be in readiness for an immediate landing. Major Macdonnell was sent on shore with a flag of truce and proposals to the governor of the fort to surrender. He returned to say that the terms were accepted. Some companies of the 78th were then landed near the fort, when the whole French garrison marched out as prisoners of war and laid down their arms in front of our line, being allowed to retain only their personal baggage, and the officers their swords. They were at once embarked and divided amongst our transports. The fort was dismantled and the guns spiked. We re-embarked, and our little fleet sailed in triumph back to Messina; but on landing we were ordered to Syracuse, and sent detachments to Augusta and to Taormina. I was with the latter, and had not been long there before I fancied myself in love with the daughter of a widow, who did all she could to encourage me and tempt me to a marriage by constantly parading a quantity of silver plate and jewels as a part of my portion ; but this chance of my imaginary good luck was soon put an end to, for I was suddenly called back to headquarters, Syracuse, and there forgot my love affair.

CHAPTER III

IN EGYPT

Expedition to Egypt—We take possession of Alexandria—Entrapped by the enemy at Rosetta—A trying retreat

IN March, 1807, we embarked as part of an expedition from Sicily under General McKenzie Fraser, destined for Egypt. We sailed from Syracuse on the 7th, arrived at Aboukir Bay about the middle of the same month, and found there a large fleet of our men-of-war and a numerous fleet of transports with the other troops of our expedition. The object of our force was to create a diversion in favour of Russia against the Turkish army in that country.

On the following morning all our light men-of-war and gunboats took up their stations as near the landing-place as the depth of the water would permit. The first division of our troops were at the same time ordered into the different ships' launches and towed by the smaller boats to the shore, a distance of at least four miles; but the weather was unusually fine. A considerable body of the enemy appeared on the sand-hill above the landing-place, but our gun-brig and gunboats soon dispersed them, and we landed without difficulty, except a good wetting as far as the knee, for the water was shallow and our boats could not get nearer than a few yards from the beach. The remainder of the troops followed in the course of the day, and landed with the same success and safety, and next morning the stores, camp equipage, and guns were landed without accident. The usual advance-guard was pushed forward, and the remainder of the troops followed in divisions, the enemy's advanced posts retiring before us, and that evening we camped, without any covering, on the dry sand, about six miles inland. Some of the enemy's cavalry were visible, but only in small numbers to watch our movements.

Next day we commenced our march for Alexandria, with very little interruption, beyond occasionally seeing large detachments of Turkish cavalry, with which our advanced guards and videttes exchanged shots and some volleys occasionally. Our advance to Alexandria continued much in the same way for a few days; we had fine weather and hot sands for our beds, with which we covered ourselves over. We felt well and slept very comfortably, and it was not till we arrived before the walls of the town that the enemy appeared in force and attempted to dispute our advance, but after a partial action and the loss of a few men killed and wounded we soon drove them before us and forced them to take shelter behind the walls of the town, and soon after the firing ceased on both sides for that day. We camped as before, beyond the walls of the old town, with our advanced piquets posted, and all other necessary precautions. It was found next morning that the enemy had evacuated the city of Alexandria during the night, and we then took formal possession, keeping most of our troops still in camp.

A force of about twelve hundred men was now told off and detached under Brigadier-General Wauchope to proceed against the town of Rosetta, on the Nile. They arrived before that place in twelve days, in safety. The general marched his men right into the centre of the town without any opposition, not even seeing an enemy, but then, being entrapped, a heavy fire was opened upon him from the tops of the houses and windows, without even the power of returning a shot. Death and confusion followed. General Wauchope was amongst the first who fell dead, and in a few minutes nearly all his detachment were either killed or wounded, and those who escaped for the moment were made prisoners and with the wounded put to death, so that only a few escaped altogether, and these found their way back to Alexandria to tell the sad and murderous tale.

This barbarous and butchering defeat required to be avenged, and a second force of about eighteen hundred men, under Major-General Sir W. Stewart, was told off for this service, in which my regiment, the 78th, was included. We marched from Alexandria late in March and arrived before Rosetta on the 7th of April, and on getting into position before the town the first thing we saw was the dead and mutilated bodies of hundreds of the former force. They were, of course, at once buried, and vengeance was the prevailing cry and feeling of the living. The late Field-Marshal Sir John Burgoyne was then a captain and our chief engineer. He at once began to throw up breastworks and other temporary defences for our guns and for the troops, these being partly completed by the next day. Some of our heavy ordnance were in battery, and commenced at once to shell the town; at the same time the enemy opened a heavy fire of artillery upon us, which was continued by both sides until dark. Rosetta is a walled town, known then to be strongly fortified. Our works were continued day and night, and additional guns got into position, until all were mounted and brought to bear on the town. The only visible good effect our cannonade produced was the cutting in two and upsetting of many lofty minarets of the mosques; we never heard the extent of their losses, but as Rosetta was full of troops and inhabitants, their casualties must have been very considerable. All our efforts failed to make any practicable breach in the walls, therefore no regular assault was attempted. Almost every evening the enemy sallied forth in large detachments of cavalry and infantry to attack our advance posts and picquets, but our troops of dragoons (ever on the watch) soon met them, and generally dispersed them; but they never gave us a fair chance, for they usually galloped off and got back to their stronghold just as we had an opportunity of destroying them.

Ten days after we commenced this siege, our good, gallant Colonel McLeod, of the 78th, was detached with five hundred men for El-Hamed, some 50 miles higher up the Nile, to check any reinforcements or surprise by additional troops coming down the Nile from Cairo to Rosetta, and our own main body continued the siege much in the same daily routine for a fortnight longer, but still unfortunately without any success in making a practicable breach in the outer walls so as to give us a fair chance of assault. All this time we were losing many brave men. It was then finally determined to raise the siege as hopeless, and to return to Alexandria. Orders to this effect were sent to Colonel McLeod, with instructions to meet us on a given day and hour at Lake Etcho; therefore, during the night of the 20th of April our batteries were dismantled and all our heavy guns spiked and buried deeply in the sand.

On the morning of the 21st our troops were under arms and formed into a hollow square, with a few pieces of light artillery and ammunition and stores in the centre. In this way we commenced our retreat for Lake Etcho. We had scarcely moved off when our square was surrounded by thousands of Turkish cavalry and infantry, howling, screaming, and galloping like savages around us, at the same time firing at us from their long muskets, but fortunately with comparatively little loss to us. We occasionally halted our square, wheeled back a section, and gave them a few rounds of shot and shell from our artillery, then moved on in the same good order. This was a long and trying day, and the only retreat in square I ever saw. It occupied us nearly twelve hours, from five in the morning till the same hour in the evening. The enemy, with fearful shouts, followed us, firing the whole of that time, but they never showed any positive determination to charge or to break our square. We were not so delicate with them, for we gave them many rounds from our guns, and when they ventured sufficiently near they were sure of more volleys than one, and we had the satisfaction of seeing numbers of them fall. We had few men killed, who were unavoidably left behind, but we were able to carry away our wounded.

CHAPTER IV

THE EL-HAMET DISASTER

Colonel McLeod's death and losses of his detachment—Captain Mackay honoured by Turkish Pasha—Return to Sicily—78th goes to England—Attack of ophthalmia

WE had soon another trial awaiting us. When we got to Etcho there was no appearance of Colonel McLeod or his detachment, nor any message from him. It was therefore at once determined to march back to El-Hamet, to ascertain his fate; and there we received information that Colonel McLeod had been attacked that morning by a large force of Turks in boats from Cairo, and the whole of his detachment destroyed, and he, that good and promising soldier, was amongst the first who fell. After a short council of war we again wheeled about and marched back to Etcho, where we camped for the night. Next day we continued our retreat to Alexandria, where we arrived without any further molestation.

Day by day several rumours reached us about our lost detachment and the gallant defence they made, but nothing positive or upon which we could rely, until the sudden appearance, six weeks afterwards, at Alexandria of Lieutenant Mathieson, who was one of the survivors, who now came to us in a Turkish dress with some proposals from the Turks at Cairo. From him we learnt that they were attacked most unexpectedly on the morning of the 21st April by a large Turkish force, who came down the Nile in boats from Cairo, on their way to Rosetta, and after gallantly resisting until more than two-thirds of their number were either killed or wounded, and the last rounds of ammunition expended, the remnant were overpowered and obliged to surrender. He also described their position at El-Hamet. Colonel McLeod and the main force were stationed on the top of a hill, and detachments of fifty, thirty, and twenty men were posted round the base, in the strongest possible places, with orders to fall back on the main body if attacked. While so posted and before daylight, the enemy landed from their boats, surrounded the hill, and at once commenced the attack. Our men fought desperately, for they expected no quarter, and numbers fell. Captain Colin Mackay with his grenadier company commanded one of the outposts, and, like all the others, fought heroically; but his two subalterns, McCrae and Christie, and nearly half his men were soon killed. He himself received a fearful sabre cut in the neck (from which, although he lived for many years, he never completely recovered) and also a severe musket wound in the thigh, both of which rendered him at once prostrate. But Mackay's spirit was not gone, for he then ordered his few remaining men to leave him to die there, and to make the best of their retreat to the headquarters; but this they would not do, declaring to a man that they would sooner die with him, than leave him. Two of his remaining sergeants then got their captain on their shoulders and succeeded under a heavy fire in carrying him off in safety to the top of the hill, and there learnt that their Colonel was already amongst the slain.

The command then devolved upon a Major Vogalson (a German); he at once wished to surrender, fixing his white handkerchief on the top of his sword, as a sign of truce to the enemy. Colin Mackay lay under a gun bleeding and suffering severely from his wound, but he happily still retained his senses, and being told that Major Vogalson wished to surrender he cried out, "Soldiers, never, never while we have a round left!" upon which they cheered him again and again, and set Major Vogalson's authority completely aside; thus they actually continued to fight until the very last round of their ammunition was gone. The enemy pressed in upon them, and after a desperate struggle they were overpowered and obliged to surrender. The Turkish Pasha who commanded, then rode up and inquired,

"Where is the brave man who has so long and so ably resisted me?" Colin Mackay, the hero of the day, was pointed out to him lying still in agony under a gun, on which Ali Pasha dismounted and, creeping near Mackay, took the sword off his own neck and shoulders and placed it gracefully on Mackay, saying, "You are indeed a brave man, and you deserve to wear my sword." From that time and long afterwards (although still a prisoner) he received the most marked attentions from the Pasha.

The few prisoners who survived were then secured, the dead were decapitated (and I fear many of the wounded also), and their living comrades were forced to carry their heads in sacks to the boats, and poor Colonel McLeod's conspicuous amongst the number. Most of the enemy then embarked with their prisoners and their trophies and returned in triumph to Cairo. There the heads of the dead were exhibited on poles for some weeks round the principal palaces of the authorities. The survivors were committed to confinement, and the officers were allowed at large on their paroles and treated well, especially Captain Mackay, who continued to receive the most marked attentions from every one. In this state they remained nearly eight months, when, after a variety of negotiations, they were exchanged and sent back to join us at Alexandria.

In another month the whole of our force left

Egypt and returned to Sicily, far from proud of the result of our unfortunate and badly managed expedition. The 78th went to Messina, and, without landing, were ordered to Gibraltar, and on arrival there were sent direct to England.

Here I must mention that during the last eight months of our inactive life in Egypt our troops suffered much from ophthalmia. I was for many months laid up from that fearful malady, from which I suffer to this day, as I have partially lost the sight of my right eye; many of our men lost one, some both eyes, and became totally blind. From that period until now I have been subject to occasional attacks of inflammation of the eyes, so bad in 1821 and 1822 that I was recommended by my medical attendants to apply for a pension. This I did through Lord Palmerston, then Secretary of War, on which I was ordered for treatment and report to Fort Pitt at Chatham, where for six weeks I was exposed to all kinds of pains and penalties. In consequence, I received a letter from Lord Palmerston saying that His Majesty was pleased to grant me the pension of an ensign, that being the rank I held when I received the injury to my sight. I wrote back to thank his lordship, but saying that, as the regulations for pensions had been changed, the amount now being allowed to increase with the rank of the individual so favoured, I still hoped, as I was now a captain, I should not be made a solitary exception to the rule. To this I received a reply ordering me again to Fort Pitt for treatment there. I remained under similar torture for another month. Soon after, I had a third reply, informing me that on the second report of the medical board His Majesty was pleased to grant me the pension of a lieutenant. I was then quartered in the Isle of Wight, so got leave of absence and went to London, determined in so good a cause to see Lord Palmerston in person. I was admitted, and then renewed my application and entreated his lordship to reconsider my case, adding that not only one eye was nearly gone but the other suffering much also. He was writing at the time and never took his pen from his paper, yet he was very kind and appeared to listen to me attentively; then, looking up, said, "I must put you on half pay, sir, if you are so great a sufferer." I said, "I hope not, my lord, while I am able to do my duty, as I have nothing else to depend upon but my commission." He then smiled and said, "Well, write to me again, and I shall see what can be done." I did so, and in due course had the satisfaction to receive a notification stating that under the circumstances of my case His Majesty was graciously pleased to grant me the pension of a captain.

But to return from this long digression to where I left my early history in the brave 78th, I proceed to say that after finally leaving Gibraltar we arrived

THE EL-HAMET DISASTER

safely in Portsmouth and marched for Canterbury, a few months after to Chichester, and then to the Isle of Wight, where we detached in companies to all parts of the island. I was sent even further with a small detachment to Selsea barracks in Sussex, to take charge of a large ophthalmic depot of that station.

CHAPTER V

THE BATTLE OF TALAVERA

Gazetted to lieutenancy in 24th Regiment—Embarked for Portugal—Battle of Talavera—Wounded—Soldiers seize Spanish pigs

I WAS not long at Selsea barracks before I wrote to the Horse Guards soliciting promotion, for I was then more than three years an ensign—an unusual period at that time. I received a sharp answer informing me that I ought to make my application through the officer commanding my regiment. This frightened me a little, for I now dreaded his displeasure also, for he was a perfect stranger to me. I had never seen him, having lately been appointed from another regiment. In a few days I regained confidence and made up my mind to write and tell my colonel frankly what I had done in ignorance of the rules of the service, and begging him to renew my application to the Horse Guards. I acted wisely, for a few weeks later I saw myself gazetted to a lieutenancy in the 24th Regiment, and being relieved of my command

THE BATTLE OF TALAVERA 31

at Selsea, I joined that corps soon afterwards in Guernsey. This was in October, 1808; after remaining there till April, 1809, we embarked for Portugal to join the army under Sir Arthur Wellesley.

After a prosperous journey I found myself again in Lisbon. The march of the 24th to join the army was by a route along the banks of the Tagus, our principal halting-places being Villafranca, Azambuja, Cartaxo, Santarem, Abrantes, and Portalegre. We halted a month at Santarem, where we were most hospitably treated by the inhabitants. There, at a large convent, the mother abbess paid us great attention, and not only entertained us occasionally with fruits and sweetmeats, but allowed us daily to visit the convent and see the nuns. There was a large hall or reception-room, where visitors assembled, in which, at the far end, there was a large grated window in an unusually thick wall; both sides of the window were barred, but sufficiently open and lighted to enable us to see through the adjoining room. The nuns appeared in twos and threes in the inner room, and in this way we chatted and made love for hours daily, but the gratings between us were so far apart that we could only reach the tips of their fingers. It was during one of these visits that the mother abbess sent a privileged servant to lay out a table with fruit and cakes, and in return for all these favours we sent our band to play under the convent walls every other evening. We left Santarem with much regret.

We joined General John Ronald McKenzie's brigade, consisting (with the 24th) of the 31st and 45th Regiments; during the months of May and June we joined many other brigades and divisions of the army. Early in July the whole British force was concentrated and reviewed on the plains of Oropesa by the Spanish general, Cuesta, who proved afterwards a worthless man and a bad soldier, and yet he was then, by gross mismanagement and perhaps by the treachery of the Spanish Government, considered senior to Sir Arthur Wellesley. Our whole army in line at that review made a grand and magnificent appearance.

It was now known that the French army under General Marmont was not very far ahead of us, and every one believed we were now concentrated and advancing to the attack. These reports were soon confirmed by facts; after a few days of marching we found ourselves on the 23rd July encamped near the river Alberche, with General Cuesta's Spanish army on our right, the town and position of Talavera de la Reina a few miles in front on the opposite side of the river, with Marshal Marmont and the whole French army not far distant facing us. It was afterwards well known that Sir Arthur Wellesley fully intended to cross the Alberche on the following morning and

THE BATTLE OF TALAVERA 33

attack the enemy, but General Cuesta overruled any such advance on the pretence that the river was not fordable. It was then suspected that the real reason for delay was to allow the enemy time to fall back on his reinforcements. On the 25th, when our advance was ordered and made, we found the water of the river only knee-deep; so we crossed, guns, cavalry, and infantry, without any difficulty, and heard that the French had actually retreated on reinforcements they expected from Madrid under King Joseph. Our main body was now halted, and in course of the day occupied the position of Talavera de la Reina; the whole of the Spanish army went on *pretending* to watch the movements of the enemy, while at the same time General Donkin's brigade and ours, consisting of the 87th and 88th Regiments, followed close upon the Spaniards with the intention of watching *them!* We halted at Santa Olalla, eight or ten miles in front of Talavera, and there took up a strong position. The Spaniards continued their advance and marched farther. On the following noon we were astounded by seeing the whole Spanish army in confused mobs of hundreds retreating past us without any attempt at order or discipline, shouting that the French army was upon us. Our two brigades immediately got under arms and formed in line ready to receive the enemy, without making any attempt to stop the cowardly fugitives, and we soon lost sight of them.

We remained firm in line till the French came well in sight; then we gave them a few volleys and retired in echelon of brigades, each halting occasionally and fronting as the ground favoured us, giving the enemy volley after volley.

This order of retreat was continued for some miles through a thickly wooded country. At last we got upon a most extensive plain, keeping the same order till the enemy affronted and opened a heavy fire, but fortunately their guns fell short, and we returned the fire with more success, and soon we saw our own gallant army drawn up in order on the heights and grounds near Talavera. This cheered us, and we continued our retreat and defence in the most perfect order. It was a most splendid sight; on nearing the main position of our army a considerable body of our cavalry advanced to meet us, and our batteries from the heights opened a heavy and destructive fire at the enemy.

Then commenced in earnest the glorious battle of Talavera, on the 27th July, 1809. The enemy made several deployments of their numerous columns during the action, attacking with desperation almost every part of our extended line, but on every occasion they failed and were driven back; yet fresh troops were brought up, the battle raged furiously, and there was much slaughter on both sides. I was slightly wounded in the thigh just as we got into our own lines. On the morning

THE BATTLE OF TALAVERA 35

of the 28th a heavy and constant cannonade was commenced, and the battle was renewed with more vigour. The French columns came on boldly and tried again and again to walk over us and break our lines, but we defied them, and at every assault they were driven back with fearful slaughter; then they advanced with fresh troops, cheering and shouting " Vive l'Empereur ! " The others, disheartened by our determined resistance, faced about with the altered cry " Sauve qui peut." The slaughter on both sides was fearful butchering work, and was continued by both armies the whole of that memorable day. Our loss in men was unusually great, and the French loss was said to be greater than ours. When the morning of the 29th dawned, not a Frenchman was to be seen ! Their whole army had retired during the night of the 28th ! leaving us the victors and masters of the field of battle.

A fearful and most distressing sight that field presented as we went over it, covered with thousands of the enemy's dead as well as our own, and thousands of wounded, numbers with their clothes entirely or partially burnt off their bodies from the dry grass on which they lay having caught fire from the bursting of shells during the action; there were many of the wounded who could not crawl away and escape. Those who still lived were at once removed, and the dead were buried. We remained on the field of battle three days more, attending to the wounded. Having then received information that Marshal Soult with the French army was at Plasencia and advancing on us, our whole army was put in retreat towards Portugal by Truxhillo, Arzobispo, and Merida, leaving the wounded and many medical officers in hospitals at Talavera. The road taken was across country, and so bad that we were obliged to employ pioneers and strong working parties to enable us to get on. From these unavoidable causes and delays, our marches on many days did not exceed ten miles, and our provisions became very limited. We had much rain, and our men suffered much from sickness, fevers, agues, and dysentery; the latter was much increased by the quantity of raw Indian corn and wild honey which the country produced, and which the soldiers consumed in spite of every threat and order to the contrary.

This retreat lasted three weeks, and I never remember seeing more general suffering and sickness. On crossing the bridge of Arzobispo we met a division of the Spanish army driving before them a herd of many hundreds of swine. Our men broke loose from their ranks as if by instinct, surrounded the pigs, and in defiance of all orders and authority, the men seized each a pig, and cut it up immediately into several pieces; so each secured their mess for that day, then again fell into place in the ranks, as if nothing had happened—this in open defiance of the continued exertions and threats of all their officers, from the general downwards. The Spaniards stood still in amazement, evidently in doubt whether they should attempt to avenge their losses, but they did not do so, and each army continued its march in opposite directions. When we camped for the night our good soldiers sent a liberal portion of their spoil to each of their officers, nor were the generals forgotten! and they, like the youngest of us, were thankful, at that time, for so good a mess. We continued our retreat by Elvas and Badajoz, then halted at various stages, and were quartered in the different towns and villages on the banks of the Guadiana for some months afterwards.

CHAPTER VI

THE BATTLE OF BUSACO

Army kindly received in Portugal—Much fighting with French army under Massena—Lord Wellington's retreat on the lines of Torres Vedras—Battle of Busaco

WE were now in Portugal, and by the kindness and hospitality of the inhabitants were made truly comfortable. We felt this change, for in Spain we were always received coolly, and got nothing in the way of food from the inhabitants upon whom we were quartered, whereas in Portugal we were received and welcomed with open arms by every one; whether rich or poor, these good people upon whom we were billeted always shared their food with us, and gave us freely of the best of every sort of provisions they had. Towards the end of this year (1809) the army was again in motion for the north of Portugal, and after a variety of marches and changes of quarters my division halted at Vizeu, Mangualde, Anseda, Linhares, and Celorico; at each of these places we had abundance of pro-

THE BATTLE OF BUSACO

visions and supplies and were, by the kindness of the inhabitants, most comfortable. Some time before this, the 31st and 45th Regiments were removed from our brigade and replaced by the 42nd and 61st Regiments.

Our troops remained inactive till about the beginning of July, 1810; then we heard that the French army, greatly reinforced, was advancing upon us under Marshal Massena. They were checked for a time by some hard fighting with our advance light division, under General Crawford, also by continued resistance of the garrisons of Ciudad Rodrigo and Almeida. The former was occupied generally by Spanish troops and some Portuguese militia, the latter fortress by one English regiment and three or four Portuguese regiments, with brave Colonel Cox, of our service, as the governor. Both these forts resisted gallantly and successfully for a short time, but after a siege of a fortnight Ciudad Rodrigo surrendered, and in ten days more the principal magazines and public buildings in Almeida were levelled to the ground by a sudden explosion, killing five hundred troops and inhabitants and destroying the principal works and means of defence; in this state of confusion and terror the brave governor, Colonel Cox, was obliged to capitulate. It was afterwards discovered that this shame and sacrifice was occasioned by the treachery of one of the Portuguese officers, who was actually the lieutenant-governor of the fort, and who openly headed a mutiny of the garrison against the governor, Colonel Cox, aided and assisted by another Portuguese officer, who was the chief of the artillery, and who had been for some time in secret correspondence with France!

The surrender of these two important strongholds encouraged the enemy to renew their advance, so that in the beginning of September Lord Wellington commenced his able and well-devised retreat on the Lines of Torres Vedras, within thirty miles of Lisbon. The Portuguese army under General Beresford and the Spaniards under the Marquis de la Romana, retreating on our flank for the same destination, all believed that we were making the best of our way to our ships for embarkation, and with the full intention of finally quitting the country. So secretly had the works of the Lines of Torres Vedras been carried on, that only rumours of their existence were heard, and those only by very few officers of high rank. It was even said that neither the English nor Portuguese Government knew anything positive about these works nor where they were constructed, and I remember well that most of our officers laughed at the idea of our remaining in Portugal, and heavy bets were daily made, during our retreat, on the chances or the certainty of our embarkation. But different

THE BATTLE OF BUSACO 41

indeed were the results, and all the world soon acknowledged the master-mind of our most noble and gallant commander.

I have said that we commenced this retreat early in September, disputing the ground daily as opportunities offered, and as we were covered by our Light Division, these brave men had nearly all the hard work and most of the fighting, but, when necessary, other troops were brought up to their support, and occasionally to relieve them from this constant harassing duty. For a few days the Portuguese militia under Colonel Trant and the Spaniards under the Marquis de la Romana were constantly kept to guard our flanks. In this way the main body, by different roads, retreated in good order for twenty or thirty miles a day, most of the inhabitants leaving their homes and property and falling back in thousands before us, rich and poor, men, women, and children, carrying little with them beyond the clothing on their backs, and halting and bivouacking in the open fields, a short distance before us, whenever the army halted for the night.

A month after we started, our division was suddenly moved off the main line of road, from the crossing of the Mondego River above Coimbra, to the mountain position of the Sierra de Busaco, some miles farther in rear of the above river and city; all the other divisions of the army were directed to the same point. Having scrambled up that mountain as best we could, our whole army was soon formed in order of battle. Below us was an extensive open but thickly wooded country, and there we saw the whole of the French army, under General Massena, advancing in many columns to attack us. The Sierra de Busaco is a very extensive range of mountains, and the main road from Coimbra, passes over the centre of it, to the interior; but in all the other places it is so precipitous and rocky, that our gallant old commander was obliged to be carried up in a blanket by four sergeants, for no horse could ascend there. By two o'clock on the afternoon of the 27th September our whole army was in position, our guns in battery, and our light troops thrown out in front for some distance. These arrangements were not long completed when the French, in different columns, advanced to attack, covered by clouds of their light troops and skirmishers. As soon as they came within range they commenced the battle with continued rounds from their numerous artillery, and our batteries returned the compliment. The skirmishers of both armies opened their fire furiously, and two of their columns pushed forward up the most easy and accessible part of the mountain with drums playing and endless cheers, and appeared as if determined to carry all before them. Our lines stood firm and retained their fire till the enemy came within easy range; they then

THE BATTLE OF BUSACO 43

gave a general volley, followed by a thundering, well-directed independent file firing, covered by our artillery, which soon made the enemy halt, stagger, and hesitate, and in a few minutes they were seen to face about and to retire in very good order. Their loss must have been great, and so was ours. At daylight on the morning of the 28th the battle was again renewed in a more extended and general way by the enemy, for they attacked simultaneously several points of our position; at the same time column after column was seen pressing up the mountain in every direction, and in one place so successfully, that at break of day one of the heaviest and largest of these actually managed to reach within a few yards of our position before it was seen by our troops. They were no sooner seen than received with a volley; yet they gallantly kept their ground, and returned our fire without ceasing for about half an hour; during that time neither of the contending lines advanced, nor gave way one inch. At last our men were ordered to charge; then the enemy retired, and, at the point of the bayonet, were driven down the hill pell-mell, in the greatest confusion, leaving many hundreds of their dead and wounded behind them. Their other minor columns of attack were repulsed in like manner. In course of that day the battle was again renewed, and the French were finally driven back, although they fought ably and with much gallantry. During this day's battle our invincible and gallant Commander-in-Chief, Lord Wellington, pulled up with all his staff in front of my regiment, and dismounted, directing one of his orderlies to do the same and to hold his horse steady by the bridle. He then placed his field-glass in rest over his saddle, and for some minutes continued coolly and quietly to reconnoitre the enemy, and this under a heavy fire!

On the morning of the 29th there was not a Frenchman to be seen. They had retired during the night, and were soon known to be moving to turn the left of our position, so as to cut off our retreat by Coimbra and the main road. But our "master-mind and head" was equal to the occasion, and in another hour the whole of our army was in retreat by a different route, to cross the Mondego River at and above Coimbra. This we did many hours before the enemy could reach us. For days we kept possession of Coimbra and the neighbouring banks of the Mondego, to give our faithful friends the inhabitants time to destroy, bury, or remove their valuables, and above all their provisions, lest they should fall into the hands of the enemy. These arrangements were made from the commencement of our retreat, and strictly carried out by the inhabitants. They left their homes and accompanied the army, taking with them only a few of their valuables. Before

THE BATTLE OF BUSACO 45

reaching Torres Vedras I remember seeing many of these noble patriots, rich and poor, all barefooted and in rags. When we finally halted they went to Lisbon. These arrangements were more distressing to General Massena than all the fighting and opposition he met with, for he was so sure of driving us into the sea, or forcing us to embark, that he left his principal magazines of provisions behind, confident of finding sufficient supplies in the country through which he passed. In all these hopes and speculations he was indeed sadly disappointed; the consequence was that they were sorely tried, and suffered much from their limited and always uncertain commissariat. We arrived at the Lines of Torres Vedras on the 10th and 11th of October, closely pursued by the enemy, their advance guards and our rear troops constantly skirmishing, and causing some loss to them and to us; but we always found time to bury our dead and carry away the wounded.

We had no sooner taken up our relative positions than we were surprised and amazed at the formidable and strong appearance of the temporary works in which we found ourselves, and which we soon learnt extended in a direct line for thirty miles from Alhandra, on the banks of the Tagus, to Mafra, on the sea coast, thus covering Lisbon completely, from the broad and deep river on one side to the wide ocean on the other, this line forming in most places a continuous chain of rising ground. My division (the 1st) was stationed at headquarters, Sobral, about the centre of the lines. By this happy chance we had an opportunity of seeing Lord Wellington daily, and of sharing his dinners occasionally, in our turn, for he made a point of asking the juniors as well as the senior officers; and dinner then, with good wine, was worth having! Yet upon the whole we fared very well, for we had a good and regular supply from Lisbon.

CHAPTER VII

THE LINES OF TORRES VEDRAS

Continued fighting—General Beresford knighted—English and French officers spend evenings together at theatres, etc. with consent of their commanders—Massena retires to Santarem

THE French were up and in position along our whole line. The next day Marshal Massena massed the strongest of his columns in front of our most formidable works, and desperate attacks were made on various parts of our line, but these, after hours of hard fighting, were always repulsed. The rest of each day was spent in staring at each other and watching the movements of the enemy, and frequently by a heavy cannonade for hours by both armies. Our loss was considerable; and from the French deserters, who were very numerous at this time, we learnt that their killed and wounded far exceeded ours, and that they were suffering much from sickness and want of provisions. In this way we remained constantly on the defensive, and frequently fighting, for upwards of four months, our army keeping our own ground and never attempting to attack the enemy, and always driving them back with much slaughter whenever they advanced to storm or carry away any of our works. During these operations the Marquis de la Romana, with his division of the Spanish army, joined us.

When we had been so employed for about two months, an authority reached Lord Wellington from England to confer the honour of knighthood on General Beresford, then the Commander-in-Chief of the Portuguese army. A general order was issued by Lord Wellington inviting one-third of the combined armies of England, Spain, and Portugal to assemble at the royal palace of Mafra, on a given day, to witness the ceremony of General Beresford being knighted, which stated that the Commander-in-Chief intended to return to his post at an early hour that night, and wished every officer to do the same, and concluded with an expression of his confidence that the remaining generals and officers of the army who were left at their posts would do their duty if attacked by the enemy during his absence. I was one of the happy ones who took advantage of this invitation, and at an early hour on the day named I started for the palace of Mafra, a distance of about fifteen miles. On our arrival there we found not only many hundreds of officers—English, Spanish, and Portuguese—but also a great portion of the Portuguese nobility, all come to do honour to the occasion, Lord Wellington and his brilliant staff amongst them; and, what was more remarkable, large masses of the French army not a quarter of a mile away from us, with their advanced piquets and sentries, were looking quietly and coolly on at our gathering, and although our visitors from Lisbon advanced in crowds as near as possible to look and stare at them in turn, not the slightest attempt was made by our brave enemies to alarm or disturb them. The same consideration and courtesy was continued during the whole of that memorable occasion, so I think to this day that the good feeling and understanding must have been previously arranged between Lord Wellington and General Massena.

As soon as the whole company had arrived, as many as could be got in were assembled in the principal hall of the palace; then appeared Lord Wellington with General Beresford on his arm, followed by a numerous suite of general officers and Portuguese nobility, and the Commander-in-Chief's personal staff. A circle was formed in the centre of the hall, into which all the grandees entered. His Majesty's commands were then read, on which General Beresford knelt down, and Lord Wellington, drawing his sword, waved it over the General's head, saying, "Arise, Sir William Carr Beresford," and ended so far the imposing pageant. Then was opened a folding door, displaying many tables laid out with a most recherché dinner and choice wines for at least five hundred people. I was one of the fortunate ones who succeeded in getting early admission. Then dancing was commenced, and kept on without ceasing until daylight. Our popular commander danced without ever resting, and appeared thoroughly to enjoy himself, though he retired at midnight, and many followed his example; but by far the greater number remained till morning, much to the delight of all the lovely and illustrious donnas and señoras of Lisbon. The night was very dark, and many officers going home lost their way and got into the enemy's lines, but on stating whence they came, were all treated most kindly, and at daylight were allowed with hearty good wishes to proceed to their respective quarters.

For many weeks after this we continued in the Lines of Torres Vedras receiving the enemy's attacks, and after many hard struggles invariably driving them back in confusion. At last Marshal Massena saw he could neither force our position, nor hope for any lasting success by continuing his efforts, so about the middle of January, 1811, being known to be sorely tried for supplies and provisions, he retreated with his army thirty miles or more, then established his headquarters at Santarem, the approach to which he at once

THE LINES OF TORRES VEDRAS   51

fortified. We followed without delay and fixed our headquarters at Cartaxo, within ten miles of Santarem, with one Light Division in front and in sight of the enemy. The remaining corps were distributed on the various roads to our right and left, following and watching the movements of our foes; and so we continued for two months, without anything important being done. Our Light Division did make some attempt to force the enemy's advance position in front of Santarem. This was a narrow causeway nearly a quarter of a mile long, built with stone and lime over the centre of an extensive bog or morass, very soft and knee-deep in water, at the enemy's end being strongly fortified with numerous covering breastworks and guns in battery; but each attack failed with considerable loss to us. For some weeks no further efforts were made in this direction, for after a long reconnaissance it was believed that the storming and carrying of such a place would entail a fearful sacrifice of life. It was then determined to make one more effort, and the three grenadier companies of my brigade were told off to lead the advance of the storming party across the causeway. For this perilous duty we marched off one morning before daylight to a certain rendezvous in a wood near the site of our intended operations. There we found, in considerable numbers, masses of infantry and many guns in battery, ready to support us, and a part of the Light Division prepared to flank our advance, by taking at once the swamps and marshes, and so clearing the way for other troops to follow with the hope of turning both the enemy's flanks and getting into their rear, while we, the storming party, at the double, with our powerful supports, should pass the causeway and storm and carry the enemy's stronghold and batteries at the end of it. All was well arranged, and willing and ready were all to make the attempt; but fortunately for many of us, just about the appointed hour for our advance it came on to rain heavily, and so continued without ceasing for some hours after daylight. As we could no longer conceal our movements from the enemy, this attack was given up, and we marched back to our quarters without any loss, but with a good wetting. Had the attack taken place our loss would have been terribly heavy.

The most happy feeling prevailed between our Light Division and the French advanced posts and garrison at Santarem. Many of our officers used to go by special invitation to pass their evenings at the theatre with the French officers at Santarem, and on every such occasion were treated in the most hospitable manner, and always returned well pleased with their visits. Of course, the sanction of the Commanders-in-Chief of both armies was given to this intimacy. The Marquis de la Romana died at Cartaxo while we were there, and was laid in state for many days, and buried with much splendour and all military honours.

While here our "patrone," the owner of our house, used to visit us very frequently. One morning, while he was present, I was sitting before the fire and poking with the tongs at the back of the chimney, when suddenly it gave way, exposing a tin box, on which "patrone" called out in alarm, " Mio dinhero ! mio dinhero ! " and at once seized it; but we insisted on seeing the contents, and found a considerable sum of money, the poor man's all, and of course we restored it to him. When the French were advancing some months before, most of the inhabitants hid their treasures much in the same way.

I was one morning taking an early walk with Lieutenant Hunt, of my regiment, in the immediate neighbourhood of Cartaxo, when we observed in a field a mule and a donkey grazing; not far off was a Portuguese peasant. I called him and asked to whom the animals belonged; he said he did not know, but that he believed they had strayed from the French lines, so I told him to drive them up to my quarters, and that I would give him a few dollars for his trouble.

CHAPTER VIII

THE LOST REGIMENTAL BOOKS

Story of the lost regimental books and the honesty of the soldiers

I MUST now tell a more creditable story. At this time I commanded a company, and had also unofficially the charge of the accounts and payments of another company, the captain having a great dislike to bookkeeping. In those days the military chest of the army was so low that the troops were frequently two or three months in arrear of pay; but the soldiers' accounts were regularly made up and balanced every month, and carried forward ready for payment when money was available. I was then sufficiently lucky to have a donkey of my own, although before this I was, like most subalterns, contented to share a donkey or mule with another officer, for the carriage of our limited baggage and spare provision; the Government allowing us forage for one animal between every two subalterns, and one ration of forage to each captain. My good and trusty beast carried two hampers covered with tarpaulin, on which was printed most distinctly my name, "Lieutenant Anderson, 24th Regiment," and in these I carried not only my few changes of clothes and spare provisions, but also my two companies' books, ledgers, etc., and at that time about two hundred dollars in cash. We had all native servants at this time; mine, a Portuguese boy, was always in charge of my baggage and donkey. The day we marched into Cartaxo, all the baggage arrived in due course except mine, and for some hours we could hear nothing of my boy nor of my donkey. At last, about dusk, he came up crying, and told me he had lost my all. I waited for many days, still hoping to hear something of my property, but all to no purpose. There were no records kept of the soldiers' accounts except the company's ledgers, so I was thus, in consequence of my loss, entirely at the mercy of my men, and had no other course left to me but to parade my own, and then the other company, and explain the situation, and my confidence in them all, and then to take from their own lips the amount of balances, debit or credit, of their respective accounts. I committed their statements at once to paper, but of course I could not say if they were correct or not. I then gave up all hope of ever seeing my lost property again.

I was advised to request the adjutant-general

of the army to circulate a memorandum in General Orders, describing my donkey and baggage, and offering a handsome reward for discovery, recovery, or for any information respecting them. A few days afterwards I received a letter from a corporal of the 5th Dragoon Guards, stationed at Azambuja, informing me that on the very evening of my loss he found my donkey feeding in a cornfield near his quarters; soon afterwards, seeing two soldiers of the 24th Regiment, he asked them if they knew Lieutenant Anderson; being told that they did, he asked if they would take charge of the donkey, to which they willingly consented, so he gave all over to them, with directions to be sure to deliver them in safety. This letter I at once took to my commanding officer, who ordered me to go without delay to Azambuja to see the corporal, and ask if he thought he could remember and identify the men. I rode off alone through a wild country, a distance of twenty miles, got to Azambuja in good time that evening, and found the corporal, whose name I cannot now remember. He expressed great surprise at my not having received the things, as more than a month had passed since he had given them over to the two men of the 24th. He said one was a grenadier and the other a battalion man, that he had not noticed them much, but thought he might be able to point them out. On this

I went to General Sir Lowry Cole and told him my story; he at once ordered the corporal to accompany me back to Cartaxo. That evening we started under heavy rain, and rode all night. The corporal was a tall and powerful man, and I must confess that I felt a little afraid of him. The night was very dark, and the ride for many miles was through a long wood. I more than once thought that if the corporal was himself the thief he might now dispose of me without any one being the wiser, so I ordered him to ride some distance in front, on pretence of looking for the road, so as to give me time for a bolt should he turn upon me. My fears proved ungenerous and unfounded, for without any accident we arrived at Cartaxo.

I reported myself to my commanding officer, who ordered the adjutant to parade the whole regiment in front of my quarters. This was done, and man after man was called in for the corporal's inspection, then passed out by a back door, without any communication with those still outside. After about a hundred had passed, the corporal, looking at the next man who entered, said, "I'll swear this is one of them." The accused became at once indignant and insolent, denying all knowledge of the charge. He was searched, and a few dollars were found between his coat and the lining, but these he said he got, like most soldiers, in course of the war.

The adjutant then proceeded to call in the remaining men; at last the corporal fixed his eyes on one of the men who entered, and said, "This is the other man; I feel sure these are the two men; I'll swear to them both." This was a private of the grenadiers, and he, like the other, boldly denied the charge. Both were then secured and sent under escort to the guard-house, and were given till twelve o'clock to make a full confession; if they did not, they would be brought to a general court-martial, and would be shot if found guilty. They both knew that such tragic ends were then by no means uncommon. They were also told the serious inconvenience and loss which their officers and fellow-soldiers had sustained, and if they would tell how the books could be recovered the commanding officer would be as easy as possible with them, and that Mr. Anderson did not care much for the rest of the things. But still they denied, swearing vengeance on the corporal. At last they saw their danger and sent for the sergeant-major and made a full confession, saying they knew there was money in the hampers, and that tempted them; they had led the donkey into a wood near Azambuja, tied him to a tree, taken the money, and buried the hampers and all their contents on the spot, and offered to show the place. I was ordered to march the two prisoners under a strong escort to the wood they mentioned, and

THE LOST REGIMENTAL BOOKS 59

there we found, still tied to the tree, the skeleton of my poor donkey, dead for at least a month. We began to dig, and soon came upon my long-lost and precious hampers, and found everything destroyed by the rain, but the books, though greatly injured, were still legible. We marched back to Cartaxo, and on arrival the prisoners were recommitted to the guard-house. My next care was to compare the verbal statements given to me by the men with the original accounts in the ledgers; and here comes the cream of my long story, and my reasons for going into this lengthy digression. To their honour, therefore, be it told, there was not half-a-crown's difference between the accounts in the ledgers and those given by each soldier from memory, the voluntary statements of no less than a hundred and fifty men! I consider this a great proof of the general honesty and integrity of the British soldier. The two prisoners were brought before a regimental court-martial, found guilty, and sentenced to corporal punishment and to be put under stoppages of pay until the money taken from me was made good. The former they suffered, but I never got back a shilling of my money. One of them died some months afterwards from wounds received at the battle of Fuentes d'Onoro, and the other was killed by another soldier in a boxing match.

We remained at Cartaxo, with the armies in

the various relative positions which I have already described, and without any great fighting, until the morning of the 7th March, 1811, when we heard that the main body of the French army had been for some days retreating, and that their headquarters, under Marshal Massena, and their rear-guard had that morning retired from Santarem.

CHAPTER IX

THE BATTLE OF FUENTES D'ONORO

Much fighting—We drive the enemy across the Mondego at Coimbra—Battle of Fuentes d'Onoro—I go into the French lines to take away the body of a friend

THE whole of our troops were put *en route* to follow them. The 1st Light Division and our headquarters and brilliant staff were all much excited, and anxious to be at them. We soon arrived at, and crossed without opposition, the formidable causeway and works which so long defied us, and which even now startled us not a little. In a few hours more we were passing through the now empty and deserted town of Santarem. We were now halted, and could not see much, but amongst the many signs of devastation and plunder we passed under the remaining walls of that once peaceful convent where, two years ago, we had spent many happy days and hours. Nothing now remained but the bare crumbling walls. The dear nuns were gone, no one knew where, most likely to Lisbon. The building was destroyed and plundered by the enemy, and we afterwards heard that such was the fate of all the convents within reach of the French during their advance towards the Lines of Torres Vedras, and that many of the nuns who had not time to escape, or who trusted to their religion and calling for protection and safety, were shamefully treated by the French officers and soldiers. Of this I can have little doubt, for when our advance was over, and we got settled amongst the inhabitants, we heard many sad stories of this description.

We had not advanced many miles from Santarem when we heard the distant firing of our Light Division and our advanced field train, now evidently up with the enemy. This went on till dusk, and we then bivouacked for the night. Next morning we were again in pursuit, without pressing the enemy, rather to allow them to get away, unless they offered battle. Their first stand was for some hours in force in front of the village of Pombal. As soon as our troops got within reach they opened a heavy fire from a numerous artillery upon us, but our troops and guns, being now well up, returned the compliment with their accustomed vigour and interest; some manœuvring and changes of position followed on the part of the French, and additional troops were shown and brought into action. Our 1st Division was then hurried to the front to support our

THE BATTLE OF FUENTES D'ONORO 63

troops, and having got into action, the fight was continued with determined valour for some time, until the enemy began to give way, and finally to retreat in some confusion. We followed them till dusk, when we halted and took up our position for the night. For days after this we had no fighting, till we drove them across the Mondego at Coimbra, and by some other bridges and fords of that splendid river, at each of which places there was a great deal of fighting.

The scenes of destruction and murder which we frequently passed in the villages and on our daily march, were dreadful. Houses and furniture burnt, men and women mutilated and murdered, lying about in the most disgusting and barbarous manner, some with their throats cut, some with their eyes and ears gone, and others cut up and most dreadfully exposed; all this for revenge, because they would not, or could not, supply the French army with provisions, and in the hope that these savage proceedings would terrify others into instant compliance. The French were suffering fearfully at that time from want of food, and their deserters to us were then unusually numerous. We had almost daily evidence of the former fact, for as we entered villages which they had left, it was an ordinary sight to see in the houses one or more dead French soldiers lying on the floor in full uniform, their arms still grasped in their hands as if asleep, also sitting in chairs with their caps on, and in full uniform, their firelocks standing upright between their legs, and quite dead; evidently they had died from want of food. I may mention that during our pursuit of the enemy we always took up our position each night in the open fields, without any covering beyond our blankets, and these were generally saturated with wet, for in Portugal rains are frequent, and dews and fogs unusually heavy during the night. If we remained for a few days or weeks we cut down some trees and bushes and made ourselves as comfortable as we could in shelters. In permanent quarters the army was always housed in the neighbouring towns and villages. When the towns and villages were deserted we were distributed among a number of empty houses and streets. The country abounded with game, especially hares, so during our idle time we were coursing or shooting with success. Each company cooked its own food, and divided it in the usual form. The officers of one or two companies messed together, giving and taking dinner with their friends occasionally. We arrived near the frontiers of Portugal driving the enemy before us, passing through Vizeu, Mangualde, Celorico, and Guarda, and some of the other villages we had occupied. The army was halted for some weeks, and many of the inhabitants joined us and again occupied their houses, but in all of these places we found the same sad evidence of the reckless destruction of houses and property of every description.

THE BATTLE OF FUENTES D'ONORO

When we reached the town of Sabugal on the Coa we found the enemy strongly posted to dispute our passage of that river. After a good deal of fighting our Light Division forced and carried the bridge, and a general engagement for some hours followed, with much slaughter on both sides. In the evening the enemy gave way and continued the retreat. It rained fearfully during the night. In the fields which my brigade occupied we were up to our ankles in mud. It was one of the most trying nights we ever had; our men suffered so much from the wet and cold that two or three were found dead on the ground when the assembly sounded next morning. Massena halted his army again in the neighbourhood of Ciudad Rodrigo and Almeida, in both of which fortresses he had a strong garrison; there he was allowed to remain unmolested for some months longer. We in like manner halted, and were put in quarters in the different villages in advance of the Coa, my brigade being comfortably housed at Alfaiates, and while here we enjoyed ourselves much in field sports and coursing. Headquarters were again near us, and Lord Wellington mixed frequently with us in the chase. Our quartermaster got sick about this time, and I was appointed to do his duty, which gave me an opportunity of improving my Portuguese. About the last week in April, 1811, the army was again put in motion to the front. Early on the morning of the 3rd of May we came in sight of the French army posted in order of battle in and beyond the village of Fuentes d'Onoro. The weather was beautiful, and both armies fought without either gaining any decided advantage. On that day the casualties on both sides were numerous, when night stopped the battle. Next morning at daylight it was renewed, and continued at various intervals in various parts of the line, until again checked by darkness. On the following morning, the 5th of May, it began again in earnest, and was more formidable and general, the numbers of killed and wounded and prisoners on both sides being very considerable. Upon the whole the French gained ground upon us, where my brigade and divisions were posted, and drove us from the village of Fuentes. This occurred about midday, and the weather being unusually hot, a suspension of hostilities was agreed upon for the purpose of carrying away the wounded and burying the dead.

I had charge of one of the fatigue parties sent on this service, and passed at once over to the village of Fuentes, then in possession of the enemy, from which they had driven us. We were received most kindly, and proceeded at once to our work of burying the dead and removing the wounded. This was continued for only an hour, when the bugles of both armies sounded "To arms!" on which the French troops near us immediately fell in, shouldered their arms, and taking off their caps,

THE BATTLE OF FUENTES D'ONORO   67

gave us three cheers. We at the same time, shaking hands with some of them, made off as fast as we could back to our own lines, and there, forming in order of battle, took off our caps and returned the same hearty good cheers. Then, and not until then, was a shot fired by either of the contending parties, and the battle again commenced with more vigour than ever, and continued with fearful slaughter until night.

Amongst our losses on that memorable day was a very dear friend of mine, Lieutenant Edmond Kelly Ireland, of the 24th Regiment. I was with him when he fell, and I knew where to find him. He was equally well loved and regretted by all his brother officers, and Lieutenants Moorsoom and Pell and I, after a talk, determined to go at once to the French lines to claim his body; so, accompanied by two of our soldiers carrying a blanket, and without leave, we moved boldly off to the French side until stopped by one of their sentries. We answered "English officers," on which he ordered us to stand still, then turned out his guard, or picquet. A French officer and a dozen men then advanced, and asked who we were and what we wanted, and being told we came to request to be allowed to look for and claim the body of an officer and friend of ours who fell that day on their ground, our brave foe said at once, "Certainly, gentlemen; give me up your swords and I shall be happy to conduct you wherever you wish to go."

We accompanied him under escort to his bush hut. He spoke freely and kindly of the battle, boasting a little that they had driven us off so much of the ground and from the village. He gave us a glass of brandy and water and biscuits, then said, "Gentlemen, I shall now conduct you where you like," so off we went to the spot where I knew poor Ireland fell. We soon recognized him amongst heaps of slain; he was lying on his back stripped of all his clothing.

He was shot right through the head, and must have died at once. We placed him in the blanket and carried him back with us, returning as we came, by the French officers' bivouac, there receiving our swords. In a quarter of an hour more we were safely back in our own lines, without having been missed. Our next work was to dig a grave, and that being damp and watery, we opened another in a higher ground, and there we laid our dear and much lamented friend. Our doings soon became known; some one told all to our colonel, who at once assembled all the officers, and gave us a most severe lecture, pointing out to us how improper and imprudent our conduct was, and how difficult it would have been, if we had fallen into the hands of a dishonourable enemy, to prove that we were not deserters, and we were cautioned not to attempt any such folly for the future. Later, we were told by one of the senior officers that, although obliged to reprimand us, no one thought more highly of

THE BATTLE OF FUENTES D'ONORO

our conduct than our good Colonel Kelly. We fully expected to renew the fight on the morning of the 6th, but to our surprise and satisfaction, as that day dawned not a Frenchman was to be seen. They retired beyond our reach during the night, and so ended the battle of Fuentes d'Onoro, fought on the 3rd, 4th, and 5th of May, 1811.

CHAPTER X

IN SCOTLAND

On sick-leave in England—In Scotland—Journey of seventy miles in twenty-four hours on foot after a ball—Appointed to assist at brigade office, 1813—Appointed captain and brigade major in the York Chasseurs

WE remained a week or more in the neighbourhood. The whole army was then again put in motion towards the south-east of Portugal, in consequence of the state of affairs previous to the battle of Albuera, under Marshal Beresford. The weather during a part of this march was very wet and stormy; our army suffered much from fever and ague. I was myself amongst the number, and was attacked so severely that after some days' suffering, without any covering or shelter, I was ordered to the rear and then on sick leave, in December, 1811, and I arrived in Plymouth in January, 1812.

My leave was for six months, which enabled me to visit my father and friends in Scotland. I was ordered to join the depot of my regiment at

Maldon, in Essex, and soon after I was sent with a recruiting party to Dornoch, in my own native country. Lieut.-General Sir David Baird was then the colonel-in-chief of my regiment, and he thought that by sending me with a party to the Highlands I might find some countrymen for his regiment; but in this both he and I were disappointed, for I remained at Dornoch four months and never got a man. I was now ordered to leave my recruiting party with an officer of the 21st Regiment and to proceed to the Isle of Wight to embark for India to join the first battalion of my regiment. This most unexpected official letter reached me while actually at a public ball; but I determined to enjoy myself for at least one night, so danced away till six in the morning, then went to bed and slept till nine, when I started on foot on a journey of seventy miles (two-thirds of which was over Highland moors and mountains) without even a path to guide me; but I was then young, and, moreover, I fancied myself in love, and that gave me heart and vigour to push on. In the last forty miles I was obliged to have a guide, and having walked the whole of that day and night, I completed my journey in twenty-four hours. I may also mention that my lady-love was at this time the acknowledged belle of all the country, but for various reasons our courtship ended in nothing beyond a sincere and friendly feeling, even to this day. I found another official letter countermanding my orders for India and directing me to return with my recruiting party and rejoin the depot at Maldon. Six weeks after this the remains of my regiment returned from Portugal and were quartered at Chelmsford, in Essex, and there we joined soon after.

General W. P. Acland commanded the district, and soon ordered an inspection of the regiment. When he came to the companies' books he was so much displeased with the irregular and imperfect manner in which they were kept that he found fault with all except Lieutenant Anderson's books, and ordered all the officers to be confined to barracks until our lieutenant-colonel could report that the books were properly posted and ready for his final inspection. This was a great triumph for me, and much good, as I shall presently show, came out of it; for in about a month England was sending a considerable force to Holland, and amongst the staff for that service General Acland's brigade-major was included. On the following day I was actually marching off in charge of our barrack guard, when an orderly arrived to say the general wished to see me at once. Another unfortunate officer was then crossing the barrack yard with his gun on his shoulder, going with others on a shooting excursion, but as he was next for duty he was ordered to get ready at once to take my place in charge of the guard, much to his annoyance. I repaired at once to the general's quarters, and on being shown in he said, "My brigade-major has been ordered away, and I want you to come and assist me at the brigade office until a successor is appointed." I thanked him, and said I should be most happy to attend and do my best. He then took me to the office and made me copy some returns; in course of the day he looked in, examined my work, and ordered me to come to him every morning. Here I must mention that beyond dining with him occasionally in my turn with the other officers of the garrison, I knew nothing of General Acland, nor he of me; but now, being nominally on his staff, I used to ride with him and dine with him more frequently, and so began to feel myself a great man, for I had much to do, having no less than six regiments and depots in the district, the reports and correspondence all passing through my hands; and my responsibilities and duties were increased by the general's frequent absence in London and other places, on which occasions he always authorized me to act in his name and to carry on all correspondence and duties as if he were present, except that if any unusual thing occurred, or any official letter arrived requiring his opinion and decision, I was to forward all such matters to his address, which he always left with me. I was also to keep his absence a secret from every one. In this way I got on most happily, when one morning he asked me, "How long have you been in this service, and what service have you seen?" I told him, and that my first battle was under him, as commanding my brigade at Maida. This seemed to surprise him, for he was not aware of my having been at Maida. He then said, "Bring me a memorandum in writing of your services." I did so on the following morning, without suspecting what use he was going to make of it. Conceive, then, my joy and surprise in seeing myself a fortnight afterwards gazetted as captain of a company in the York Chasseurs. Of course, I thanked my benefactor with all my heart and soul; but he only said, with his accustomed kindness, "You deserve it, and I hope you will get on." This was not all, for he next applied to the Horse Guards to have me permanently confirmed as his brigade-major; but that was refused on the ground that I was appointed to a new regiment where experienced officers were immediately required, and therefore I must join at Sandown barracks in the Isle of Wight with as little delay as possible. Still, he kept me for some weeks longer with him. At last the time came when I was obliged to leave. He then asked me to write to him occasionally, but he lived only for three years after. I did write repeatedly, and as often heard from him, and it is in fond and grateful acknowledgment of my much-lamented friend that I gave my dear son the name of Acland. Had I never seen General Acland I would not have been a captain for ten years or more.

On joining the York Chasseurs at Sandown barracks I was pleased at finding the officers a fine set of young fellows, all promoted from other regiments for their services or strong family interest. Lieut.-Colonel Coghlan was a smart, experienced officer, very kind to all, but a strict disciplinarian; and as there was no end to our parades, we soon became a most efficient regiment, and the most united and happy corps of officers I ever knew.

CHAPTER XI

VOYAGE TO BARBADOS

Portsmouth—Guernsey—Sail for Barbados—Honest Henry—Frightful storm—Adventure at Funchal

I HAD the good fortune to see at Portsmouth the Prince Regent of England, the Emperor of Russia, the Emperor of Austria, the King of Prussia, the Duke of Wellington, Marshal Blücher, Marshal Beresford, Lord Hill, Lord Combermere, Prince Esterhazy, Contezoff, and many more distinguished English and foreign officers, all in uniform, and covered with their brilliant stars and orders. This was immediately after the first occupation of Paris and the declaration of peace. It was a glorious day, and all the world was there to see them. A few months afterwards we embarked for Guernsey, and remained there till October of the same year, when we embarked for Barbados.

Our residence in Guernsey was more than usually gay. There were several other regiments of the line stationed there at the same time, and the people of the town and neighbourhood were more than hospitable, for we had constant dinner-parties and public and private balls. The young ladies were more than usually numerous, and very many of them very beautiful. In such a society, and with such luring temptations, it cannot appear a matter of wonder that most of our young men were, or fancied they were, desperately in love; and to encourage our pretensions our kind and ambitious colonel (who was himself a married man) at every ball slyly hinted to the elderly ladies and mothers, as his officers passed near, "That is the nephew or cousin of Lord So-and-so," and "That is a young man of considerable property in the West Indies," and so on, in the most seductive manner, until he made us all out to be men of substance and wealth. How far this marvellous information was believed I know not, but it did not in any way lessen the continued friendship and hospitality which we invariably received. Every evening after dinner carriages from our friends assembled in front of our mess-room, and as the constant use of these caused many of us to be absent from parades on the following mornings, with the consequent displeasure and reprimand from our colonel, we used to allow them to remain stationary for some time after the appointed hour for our departure, knowing well that our colonel (who lived opposite our messroom) was watching us all the time, and that, although he did pitch into us for being absent from his parades, he was nevertheless as anxious for our enjoyment and fun as we were ourselves; therefore we pretended to show no desire to be off, until this mock indifference brought our kind commander over and in amongst us, saying, "Gentlemen, gentlemen, you are late: why are you not off?" On this one of our captains (Parker), who was for many years private secretary to his Royal Highness the Duke of Kent and a man of courteous address, used to get up and say, "Really, colonel, you are very good, but we have determined not to go to any more parties for fear of being late for parades in the morning." Then he would answer, "Pooh, pooh! d—n the parades; you must all go—you must all go." And so we started for our rooms and dressed and were off as usual. So long were our dancing and parties continued that most of us were again absent from parade the following morning. Our colonel still continued to send sergeants to town to look for us, and to say he wished to see us immediately. Soon after that, Captain Parker followed alone to smooth the way and to prepare for our reception. This he effectually did by his well-timed excuses and his courteous manner, so that when we arrived in barracks the colonel was so perfectly satisfied that he only said he was glad to hear that we enjoyed ourselves so much. This was latterly almost an everyday occurrence, and I mention it here to show how happy young men may be under a good and kind colonel.

But all things must have an end, and so had our fun in Guernsey; for, as I have already said, we all embarked in October for Barbados, leaving our sweethearts and friends without coming to any positive understanding as to the future. On our voyage we called at the Cove of Cork, where we remained for some days, and were then joined by the 40th Regiment in transports, bound for the West Indies and finally for New Orleans, and here our good and much respected friend Colonel Coghlan left us and retired on half-pay.

I was at this time in command of one of our transports, and here must notice an instance of true honesty that occurred. Being tired of visiting the Cove, I agreed with some officers to take a run up to Cork for a day or two; but, before leaving my ship, I gave orders to the senior officer not to allow any of the men to go on shore. On my return to the Cove I met some of the officers, who told me that my servant had deserted, having got leave to land on the pretence of taking my clothes to be washed. This alarmed me not a little, for I had then between three and four hundred pounds belonging to the troops and to myself in one of my trunks, in dollars and doubloons, and as I entrusted my servant, whom I had long known, with my keys, I now made sure all was gone; I hurried on board and found the door of my cabin locked, and, inquiring for the key, an officer handed it to me, saying my man Henry gave it to him with a request to let no one have it except his master, should I return before he did. I instantly opened my cabin, and the first thing I observed was my bunch of keys hanging by a piece of twine from the top of the berth; I seized them with a trembling hand and heart, and instantly opened the money trunk, and on counting my bags and treasure, to the honour of poor Henry be it told, not one dollar was missing. Poor, honest Henry was never afterwards heard of by me, and I was glad he had secured his escape, for had he been captured and brought back he must have been severely punished.

We finally sailed from the Cove of Cork escorted by a line-of-battle ship and two small men-of-war, and for a day or two made good progress; but we were then caught in a severe gale, right against us, and after struggling for a day or two the sign was made by our commodore to return to "port in view," namely Bantry Bay, on which all the fleet put about, and, led by the line-of-battle ship, steered direct for that safe and splendid anchorage, which is very extensive within, but narrow and dangerous at its entrance, so that not more than one ship can enter with safety at a time. As we were passing in, one of our fleet, the *Baring* transport, with the 40th Regiment on board, got so near the rocks that she struck, and immediately after went broadside on, and finally became a total wreck. My ship followed in her wake and passed within fifty yards of the stranded vessel, and it being then early in the day, it was most distressing and heart-rending to see the sufferers all in confusion crying for help, which from our position it was quite impossible to render, for we were obliged to run in, in order to save ourselves. So was every other ship as she reached and entered the same narrow passage. But the men-of-war and other vessels which had got safely into the bay soon sent their boats to the rescue, and all the soldiers and crew, excepting about fifteen wretched men, women, and children who were drowned in their hurry to jump on the rocks, were saved, but the ship and nearly all the baggage and cargo were lost. I remember as we passed the ill-fated ship seeing an officer's wife standing and screaming on the poop, her infant in her arms, and with no covering beyond her nightdress; I heard afterwards that the child fell out of her arms and was drowned, but she herself was saved. The survivors were encamped on the beach for some days, and then were divided for a time amongst the other transports, on which the whole fleet again returned to the Cove of Cork to charter another vessel for the sufferers.

About a week after that we sailed once more for our destination. The weather was fair and beautiful until we arrived off Funchal, in Madeira, and thence we had a dead calm. Some of my brother officers from another ship came on board, and being, as we supposed, close in to the town, we proposed after dinner to go on shore. We had a lieutenant of the navy as agent of transport in charge of us. As he made no objection to our landing (believing the calm would continue until the following morning) our captain consented, and ordered two boats to be manned, so eight of us started on the clear understanding that we should return by daylight next morning. Our sailors, who were promised all sorts of drinks and rewards, pulled most heartily, but the distance to the shore proved much further than we expected, and a dark night overtook us; but still we pushed on, and the brilliant lights in the town cheered us. At last we reached the beach and found a heavy surf running in, and none of us knew the proper place for landing; but the sailors, undaunted, assured us there could be no danger, so one of the boats (not mine) took the lead, and was no sooner in the surf than she was instantly upset and all her passengers were seen struggling in the sea; but after a good ducking they all got safe on shore, and also managed to secure their boat.

My sailors wanted to try the same risk, but I would not allow them. Seeing a shore battery near us, we approached, and were challenged by a Portuguese sentry, and answered, "English officers, who request to be allowed to land." This the sentry refused, and said his orders were to allow no one to land. My knowledge of the language was now of some use to me, and after talking to the sentry quietly and kindly and promising him a dollar, the brave man suffered us at once to step on shore, and showed us the way to the town. There we found our friends, still dripping wet, but with some good wine before them. After refreshing ourselves a little, we went to look after our boats and sailors, and found all safe. We then gave them sufficient money to make them comfortable, and urged them to leave one man at least as sentry over the boats. This they promised to do, so we returned to our hotel, determined to have our fun also. Soon after this the weather from a calm suddenly changed to a strong wind and heavy rain, which continued to pour without any change during the whole night. This damped our follies, but we were up and at our boats before daylight next morning. These we found all safe, but not a sailor to be seen anywhere; and when daylight appeared not one of our ships was in sight. This was truly distressing and alarming, but we had still hopes of seeing and overtaking our fleet, for beyond the town, and in our course, a long promontory of land projected, sufficient to conceal our ships from us, even if they were close behind that obstruction.

Without further delay we searched for our

sailors and eventually found them, but in such a state and humour from drink that they positively refused to go to their boats, or any farther with us, saying that we all had been dry and enjoying ourselves, while they were left hungry and wet watching the boats. All our coaxing and entreaties had no effect, and they got worse and worse and even insolent. At last large promises of grog and money when we should reach our ships made some impression on the best of them, and after many more oaths and much grumbling, the others at last consented to go with us, still believing our ships could not be far beyond the distant point. Our next care was (having had no breakfast) to get some cold meat and bread and a couple of kegs of good wine. Our boats were then launched, and off we started with three cheers. It took us two good hours to pull round the point; then came our great fear and alarm, for although the wide ocean was then clear as far as the eye could reach, only one solitary ship was to be seen, and that nearly hull down, in our direct course. Here the sailors again declared they would not go one yard farther. Much conversation and many arguments followed, and for a time we did not know what to do. To go back to Funchal would be our ruin, and risk perhaps our commissions; moreover, all our money was gone, and as we were strangers we did not know where to get more. At last great promises were renewed, and after another and another tumbler of wine our mutinous crew consented to try to make the ship in sight. Fortunately the weather was moderate, and we had a light breeze in our favour; by good luck, also, we had a few empty bags in our boats, which were intended to carry off some vegetables to our ships; with these the sailors managed to rig out some sails fixed upon oars; this assisted them very much in their pulling, yet with all their struggling and endless swearing it was not till four in the afternoon that we managed to reach the ship, which we hoped to be our own, but, alas! we were again disappointed, for she proved to be an American whaler; but we were received most kindly, and provided at once with a good dinner.

From her deck another ship was in sight, about ten miles distant, which the American captain assured us was one of our own convoy, and that he had observed her all day, as our fleet went by, trying to remain as much as possible behind, on the pretence of making repairs. This was cheering, if we could but get our men to take again to their boats. At last we prevailed, and off we started, the American captain giving us a small cask of water and some rum to cheer us; and at seven o'clock that evening, after a trying exposure and fatigue of eleven hours, we reached the sail in sight (which proved to be our ship) in safety, thankful indeed for our escape from the tremendous danger to which we had so foolishly exposed ourselves. Had it come on to blow hard at such a distance from the land, the chances were that we must have perished or been starved to death from want of provisions. When we got on board our fleet was just visible ahead from our decks, and it took us two days under all sail to make up with them.

CHAPTER XII

ST. VINCENT AND GUADELOUPE

Life in Barbados—I am appointed acting-paymaster—President of a court-martial—Deputy judge-advocate—At St. Vincent—Expedition to Guadeloupe—Appointed deputy assistant quartermaster-general and sent to Guadeloupe

WE had no more mishaps during that voyage, and got safely to Barbados on December 14, 1814. We landed on the following morning, and occupied St. Anne's barracks, and the same evening dined with the officers of the 80th West India Regiment. None of us had been in the West Indies before, so that everything was new to us. Nothing attracted my notice so much as the imposing display of well-dressed negro servants who attended at dinner; most of them were boys, but very efficient and up to their work. The lights, all in glass shades (for all the windows were open), were also more than usually brilliant, and the dinner and wines excellent. As to dessert, it was in profusion, with countless fruits which we had never before seen. We spent, indeed, a happy night, and our first impressions from all we saw, and the kindness and hospitality with which we were received, gave all a charming and contented hope of a continued happy residence in the West Indies.

There were no less than four more regiments of the line in Barbados at that time, so that each succeeding day we were more and more entertained and fêted. The garrison was then very healthy, and we began to think ourselves in good quarters and the climate not quite as bad as all the world represented it to be. For weeks and weeks we got on very well, and without much sickness. At last a gradual change took place, and we began to lose men daily, and soon the numbers increased, the prevailing complaint being yellow fever, which also attacked the other regiments in garrison. We were the last comers, and lost considerably more than any of the other regiments. Amongst our dead was our paymaster, Captain Thompson. His death occasioned a committee of paymastership to be appointed, of which I was the junior member, and as the others disliked the work, I engaged, with the consent of my commanding officer, to do all, and consequently I got the whole of the allowances, namely, nine shillings per day in addition to my pay. I also continued to do my regimental duties.

About this time I was appointed president of

a garrison court-martial. The case was one of much difficulty and complicated evidence, but we got through it, and the proceedings were forwarded to Major-General Robert Douglass (then Adjutant-General to the Forces in the West Indies and commanding the garrison), by whom they were at once approved, and nothing more was heard on the subject till a fortnight later, when, to my surprise, I saw my name in General Orders as deputy judge-advocate-general! I immediately wrote to General Douglass thanking him for the appointment and stating that I should endeavour to fulfil the duties to the best of my powers. On the following morning I received the more than flattering answer as follows:—

"SIR,—In appointing an officer to perform the important duties of Deputy Judge-Advocate it was my duty to select a competent one, and I am satisfied I have done so.
"I have the honour to be, etc., etc., etc.,
"ROBERT DOUGLASS,
"*Major-General and Adjutant-General.*"

The first case for trial in my new appointment was unfortunately that of a captain of my own regiment (for being drunk on duty). He was found guilty and cashiered, but strongly recommended to mercy on account of his former services, and this recommendation from the court induced His Majesty to allow him to retire from the service by the sale of his commission. After this I had occasion to see General Douglass repeatedly, but, as he was a very reserved man and at all times a very strict disciplinarian, I had no intimacy with him then beyond our formal meetings; however, as I shall hereafter show, we became intimate soon afterwards.

The York Chasseurs were removed to the island of St. Vincent, and we had not been many months there under our new Lieut.-Colonel Ewart, when General Orders reached us from headquarters (Barbados) detailing an expedition then ordered from the various islands in the command to be immediately formed to proceed against the islands of Martinique and Guadeloupe, and to rendezvous in the first instance at the small group of islands called the "Saints." The York Chasseurs were included and attached to Major-General Campbell's brigade, and all the staff appointments were filled except that of brigade major. Our senior captain at this time was Holland Daniel, a distant relative of Sir Henry Torrens, then Adjutant-General to His Majesty's Forces at the Horse Guards, and from whom my friend Holland Daniel brought out letters to our Commander-in-Chief, Lieut.-General Sir James Leith, who was also an officer of some service with the 61st Regiment in Spain and Portugal, so that when the General's orders appeared with the staff

ST. VINCENT AND GUADELOUPE

vacancy which I have named, Captain Holland Daniel made sure he would be the fortunate man to fill it. In a few days our transports arrived, and we embarked and sailed for the appointed rendezvous, and there found a considerable number of troops already arrived; and several ships-of-war, with the admiral and Sir James Leith, and other transports with troops were standing in. As soon as we got to anchor Colonel Ewart went on board the admiral's ship to report his arrival, and on returning in his boat we observed him standing up and waving a paper over his head. We at once believed this to be good news, and on reaching the deck he said: "Anderson, you are the lucky man; you were appointed major of brigade, but in justice to myself and my regiment I have been obliged to object to your leaving me, and I have done so, with the assurance to the Commander-in-Chief and to General Douglass, who recommended you, that no one rejoiced more than I at your good fortune, and that I objected to your leaving me solely on the grounds of your being one of the few officers of my regiment who ever saw service, and to whose experience, therefore, I attached the greatest importance, as we were now sure of going into action. I told the Commander-in-Chief that I had the highest opinion of you as an able and intelligent officer, and that I should be willing to part with you when the fight was over should his Excellency then see fit to give you any other staff appointment."

All this was very gratifying, yet very galling, for staff appointments are not so easily had, but I could not do less than thank him for his good opinion and patiently bear my fate. Ewart saw my distress and said: "Come, I must take you on board the flagship and introduce you to the Commander-in-Chief." So off we started, but on getting on board Sir James Leith was so engaged that he could not see me, but General Douglass received us, and Colonel Ewart went again kindly over his objections and said much more to please and flatter me. General Douglass said that I must remain for the present with my regiment, and that he was glad to hear such a good report of me. We then took leave and returned to our own ship.

During that and the following day the whole of the troops of the expedition arrived, and about the same time a frigate came from England bringing the news of the battle of Waterloo, the abdication of Bonaparte, and the restoration of the Bourbon dynasty to the throne of France. This great and astounding news was at once dispatched under a flag of truce by the admiral, Sir Charles Durham, and Sir James Leith to the respective governors of Martinique and Guadeloupe, with the earnest request that they would at once acknowledge and show their loyalty to Louis XVIII, their now reigning King, and thus put an end to our intended hostile proceedings and useless effusion of blood. The governor of Martinique at once acknowledged the sovereignty of the Bourbons, and hoisted the white flag, but General Boyer, of Guadeloupe, returned an answer that he did not believe one word of the news, and that he was determined to fight for his Emperor and to resist to the last.

On the following morning, the 9th of August, 1815, our armament sailed from the Saints in two divisions for Guadeloupe, the main body of the force under the Commander-in-Chief for Grande Ance Bay, and one brigade, consisting of the 63rd Regiment and York Chasseurs under Major-General Douglass, for Bailiffe. In a few hours the whole were landed in safety at these places respectively. Our landing at Bailiffe was opposed by a considerable number of French infantry, but we had a man-of-war with us, which covered our landing and cleared the beach for a sufficient distance to enable us to get on shore safely. The enemy formed again at a little distance inland, and there we at once attacked them, and finally drove them before us till they reached Basse Terre and got under the protection of the batteries of Fort Matilda, beyond which we took up our position for the night, expecting to be joined by our main body next day. In the course of this day we lost some men, but no officers except Captain Lynch of the 63rd. The main body of our troops was also opposed on landing, and constantly during this march of two days from Grande Ance to Basse Terre, but their casualties were not numerous, and they joined us in safety at the expected time. Guns were then put into position, and they began battering the town, the fire being ably returned from Fort Matilda. Preparations were at the same time made by us for storming, and when the proper time arrived a flag of truce was sent in, giving the enemy the choice of surrendering without risking any further additional loss of life. This the governor refused, but the French general officer, who was next in authority, at once complied. He hauled down the tricolour and hoisted the white flag, acknowledging all as prisoners of war. The 63rd and some more of our troops marched in and took possession, the French garrison having first marched out under arms and laid them down in front of our main force, which was drawn up in line ready to receive them. The French troops, as prisoners of war, were formed in separate divisions and marched back to town into separate places of confinement until ships were ready to receive them, which finally took them back to France. The officers were allowed to retain their swords, and both they and the men were allowed to keep their private baggage. The governor, General Boyer, was nowhere to be found, till after a long search he was discovered concealed in a wine-cellar, determined to the last to uphold the honour of his Emperor. Of course, he was treated with every kindness, and was sent with the others to France.

A week afterwards the whole of our troops were re-embarked and went back to their former quarters in the different islands, except the 25th Regiment, which was left to garrison Basse Terre and Guadeloupe, and the latter was now made the headquarters of the British troops in the West Indies. I returned with my regiment to St. Vincent and continued my additional duties as acting paymaster, expecting nothing better for some time. In a few weeks the General Orders arrived, and to my great delight and surprise I read: " Captain Joseph Anderson, of the York Chasseurs, to be Deputy-Assistant Quartermaster-General to the Forces, and to repair forthwith to Headquarters, Guadeloupe." I was indeed proud of my extraordinary good luck, and so was Colonel Ewart, and as a mark of his regard he made me a present of a handsome staff sword, which he had himself worn for many years in a similar appointment. I soon handed over my company and my accounts as paymaster to officers appointed for those duties, and availed myself of a passage in the very first vessel that started for Guadeloupe, and arrived there safely.

CHAPTER XIII

DOMINICA

Sent to Dominica—A fatal foot-race—I give up appointment and rejoin my regiment at St. Vincent—An awful voyage

COLONEL POPHAM, of my old regiment, the 24th, was then deputy-quartermaster-general and the head of my department. He was always on the staff, and had not served much with the 24th during my time, so that I was very little known to him; but he received me most kindly, and set me at once to work in his office at correspondence and various public returns, which gave me a good idea of the duties. Thus I continued more than a month, until at last, being considered up to my work, I was sent off to Point à Pitre, thirty miles from Basse Terre, to take the sole charge of that station, or rather of the duties of the department, for there I found Colonel Brown as commandant with his 6th West India Regiment. A more charming man and able officer I have seldom or ever met. I became a member of the mess, which was well conducted and most comfortable. Although we had little society at Point à Pitre, I found enough to do, and spent my time very happily there for some months.

I was then suddenly ordered to hand over my charge to Captain Killy Kelly, of the 6th West India Regiment, and to proceed to Roseau, in the island of Dominica, to take charge of the department there, and I found the change a very agreeable one. The governor at the time, Colonel Maxwell, was a most kind and hospitable man, and I lived within a few yards of Government House. There was a very extensive and pleasant society amongst the residents and settlers in the town of Roseau and its neighbourhood. Parties and dinners were frequent, and I enjoyed them very much; but, alas! our greatest pleasures are subject to change, and ours had a partial check which proved very distressing to many. I was dining with a large party at Government House, and amongst the guests was a Dr. de Ravière. The conversation turned on foot races, and he boasted much of his powers and success in that line. I had had some experience in running also, and asked him what odds he would give me in a thousand yards. He declined giving any odds, and so we agreed to run equal for two hundred dollars. A place and day was at once appointed. At the given day and hour (three in the afternoon) no less than four thousand people had assembled, lining each side of the road we were to run. Tents and marquees were pitched for our dressing and for refreshments. Amongst the spectators were Dr. de Ravière's two lovely sisters. We soon appeared, both dressed in flannel, and the word being given we started. I allowed him to lead for twenty yards, then pushed on, and for a few yards we ran abreast; then I passed him, increasing my advantage. He (in trying to overtake me) fell down, and became for a time almost insensible. He was carried home and put to bed; fever soon followed, and next day he was dead. In the absence of a medical man a Major Jack undressed me and put me into a tub of rum as a bath, then to bed, giving me a mixture of brandy and porter till I became almost unconscious, and finally fell into a sound sleep, from which I did not awake till next morning. I was free from fever, but was confined to my bed for that and the following day, and was kept ignorant of the fate of Dr. de Ravière for some days longer. It was indeed a foolish frolic to attempt to run a thousand yards in such a climate and at such an hour.

I remained at Roseau for some months after, with an excellent house and good allowances, amounting in all to more than double my regimental pay. Early in 1817 orders arrived from England for the removal of the York Chasseurs from the Windward and Leeward Islands to

Jamaica, a distinct and separate command. I was then written to, officially, to say that my staff appointment would be continued if I exchanged into another regiment within that command, but if not I must follow the York Chasseurs to Jamaica in command of a detachment of the regiment still remaining at St. Vincent. This was a serious step for me to decide on, and I took some days before I finally made up my mind. I was then the second captain of my regiment, and to exchange into another would place me at the bottom of the captains, and yet my appointment was a most important and lucrative one, and such as I might never again hope to enjoy. For days I was quite undecided and did not know what to do, but at last I thought the least risk and the best chance of promotion was to give up my appointment and to follow my regiment. I wrote to the adjutant-general (my friend General Douglass) accordingly, and in due course I saw my name in General Orders directing me to hand over the charge of the quartermaster-general's department and to join a detachment of my regiment at St. Vincent.

The first opportunity was from Barbados, from which island I knew I could readily get a passage to St. Vincent. I left Dominica in a small colonial schooner, the *Johanna*, commanded by a mulatto and manned exclusively by negroes. Our captain knew nothing of navigation, but was in the habit of making this voyage successfully by taking his departure from Point des Salines, in Martinique, and steering direct east, against the trade winds, for a day or two, to clear the islands, and then due south, with a man at the mast-head to look out for Barbados, which is a very high land. In clear weather it is seen at a distance of fifty-nine or sixty miles, but we had thick fogs and much rain, so that though we cruised about with a man constantly at the mast-head for some days, we could nowhere discover the island nor any other land. In despair our captain turned back before the trade winds, sure of making some of the islands, from which he could again take a fresh departure. About sunset we recognized Martinique, and on the following morning Point des Salines once more, from which we again took our departure; but that effort proved worse than the former, for on the second day we were opposed by a fearful hurricane, which carried away both our masts, and left us a helpless, unmanageable hulk in a wild and terrible sea. Our situation became indeed most fearful and alarming. The sea was constantly breaking over us, and wherever there was any opening it rushed in tons below, until the cabin, where I was alone, was completely flooded by many feet of water. All the crew except the captain gave up in despair, and shut themselves up below, crying and moaning all the time. The captain manfully kept to the deck, lashing himself to the tiller ring-bolts. In this perilous situation we continued for two days and one night, expecting every moment to be our last, for our ill-fated barque, being under no control, was tossed about at the mercy of the raging seas. We gave up all hope—then, recommending ourselves to Providence, we expected every moment to founder. In this awful and long-continued danger I must confess my mind was much troubled about a few hundred pounds which I had on board with me, in doubloons and dollars, and which I sorely grieved to think my sister would now lose. On the second day of this hurricane a sail appeared in sight (or rather a vessel under almost bare poles). It soon passed near us, and our captain managed to show his ensign on a spar upside down, expecting that the stranger would try and come to our assistance; but instead of doing so, he hoisted his own flag reversed, and continued his course. Although this was an English man-of-war, she was in such distress and danger in this heavy gale and raging sea that it was quite impossible for her to come near us or to render any help.

Towards the evening of the following day the storm moderated, and by great exertions our people managed to rig up something like a jury-mast, on which they hoisted one or two of the smaller sails, and we bore away before the trade wind, sure of making some of the islands which we knew must be to leeward. In the evening land was seen ahead, but the sea was still running so high that our captain was afraid to go too near it, and so kept an offing as he best could until next morning. Then at daylight we steered for the land; in a few hours we were satisfied that it was the island of St. Lucia, and about noon we got to the anchorage, with our lives at least in safety, and truly thankful, indeed, for our marvellous escape from death. I took my final leave of the schooner *Johanna* and landed at once, and here I found my friend General Douglass acting-governor of the island. I dined with him, and on the following day, with his advice, took my passage in a small vessel bound direct for St. Vincent, where I arrived in safety, and took command of the detachment of my regiment, then under orders for Jamaica.

CHAPTER XIV

AN AMUSING DUEL

Jamaica—Return to England—York Chasseurs disbanded—
Trip to France—An amusing duel

I HAD not been many days at St. Vincent before the papers announced that no less than sixteen vessels had foundered in the late hurricane, and as none of the crews were heard of it was taken for granted that they must have all perished. I soon afterwards left St. Vincent with my detachment, and after a pleasant voyage arrived in safety at Port Royal, Jamaica. On the following day I landed and joined the headquarters of my regiment at Stony Hill barracks. The change from staff to regimental duties I did not much like, but there was no help for it. I found myself again associated with my gay and happy brother officers, with Major Dumas in command, Colonel Ewart having gone on leave. Some months afterwards four companies of the regiment were detached and sent under my command to Falmouth, Montego Bay, Marroon Town, and Savanna-lamar, my station being at the former of these places. Our barracks there and at all the other stations were very good and we enjoyed ourselves very much. For nearly two years we were quartered in that part of Jamaica. My orders were to visit each detachment occasionally, which I did repeatedly, not solely as a point of duty, but also for my own amusement.

About the month of March, 1818, our senior major arrived from England and took command of the regiment at Stony Hill; Major Dumas joined us at Falmouth, and relieved me of my charge. I now began seriously to think of a trip to England, for my health was not particularly good and I required a change. On consulting our assistant-surgeon, he advised me to apply for a medical board, so I wrote officially to Major Dumas, who forwarded my application to the deputy adjutant-general at headquarters, Kingston, and by return of post I was advised to repair to Stony Hill, to appear before a medical board. I made that journey, a hundred and twenty miles overland, on horseback in four days. I appeared before the board, who, without asking me any questions, recommended me for twelve months' leave of absence to England. We sailed from Port Royal early in April, and touched at Havana, where we remained ten days, shipping at night (contrary to the laws of the port but with the connivance of the governor) thousands and thousands of dollars and doubloons on account of merchants in England, upon which our admiral and his senior officer had a large percentage. We left Havana, and arrived in England early in May, 1818, after a most agreeable passage. The admiral and his captain were particularly jolly, and very kind to us all; the former had the officers of the wardroom daily at dinner in their turn, and entertained us with his numerous stories; among other things he told us he had made a hundred thousand pounds during his three years' command on the Jamaica station.

Again in England, and with my health much improved by the voyage, I endeavoured to enjoy myself as much as I could. About December, 1819, I heard that the York Chasseurs were ordered from Jamaica to Canada, to be there disbanded, consequent upon the general peace which followed the battle of Waterloo and the great reductions in the British army. Soon afterwards I received an official letter informing me that I was to consider myself on half-pay in three months from that date. This was indeed bad and most unexpected news for me, but I endeavoured to make the best of it, consoling myself with the hope of getting employed again as soon as possible by an appointment to some other regiment, and in this mind I returned soon afterwards to London, determined to see what chances I had at the Horse Guards. After waiting some time I attended the levée of the Military Secretary, Lieut.-General Sir Henry Torrens, and stated my case, and my anxiety to be employed. He received me with his usual consideration and kindness, and directed me to write to him on the subject. I did so in due course, and soon received his answer saying that on my stating my readiness to proceed to Sierra Leone I should be appointed to a company of the 2nd West India Regiment. I immediately wrote back saying that my health was still very indifferent, from my services in the West Indies, but that rather than forfeit all hopes of employment I would proceed to Sierra Leone, should his Royal Highness the Commander-in-Chief wish me to do so. This was a decision forced on me, and anything but satisfactory to my feelings, so with fear and trembling I watched every succeeding gazette which appeared for the next month, expecting to see myself appointed to the 2nd West India Regiment, but to my joy no such notice appeared then or afterwards, and I again began to breathe freely and hope for something better.

Months of idleness passed in London, and as I was afraid to appeal again to the Horse Guards for a time, I determined to go at once to France to study the language, for I well remembered how much inconvenience I had suffered while in the French island of Guadeloupe from not being able to speak French fluently. Fortunately, at this time I was in correspondence with a dear friend and brother officer, Lieutenant Wharton of the York Chasseurs, and I persuaded him to accompany me to France. Having made our arrangements, we left London early in 1820 for Southampton, where we took our passages in a sailing mail packet for Jersey, and from thence to St. Malo in Brittany, and there, for the first time, I found myself in "la belle France." Next morning we went up the St. Malo river, in a passage boat, for about twenty miles to Dinan, and having procured good lodging, we remained there for nearly a month, then started on foot, determined to make easy stages in the same way until we reached Nantes. After our second day's travelling we found ourselves tired and done up, so we rested a day, and on the following morning took our seats in the diligence direct for Nantes. Here we managed to get most comfortable lodgings with a widow named Fleury and her two pretty daughters, who provided us with our breakfast in our own English fashion. We became members of a most excellent table d'hôte, where we met many French officers belonging to the regiment then in garrison, and with whom we soon became intimate, for we told them we were officers, and had had the honour of having been opposed to them.

In February, 1821, I returned to London,

stopping for a few days *en route* with a friend at Boulogne-sur-Mer. This was Dr. McLaughlin, whom I knew in Portugal as a staff assistant-surgeon, who attended me while sick at Lisbon. His name being now before me, reminds me of him as a gay young fellow who, one morning at Lisbon, went to visit another assistant staff surgeon named McDermot, who was not at home when he called, but he saw his landlady, a handsome young widow, and, if the account be true, he attempted to kiss her; at least, so she told her lodger on his return home. McDermot at once called on McLaughlin and begged him to make her an apology. This he refused, saying he took no improper liberties, and saw no necessity whatever for an apology, and laughed at the very idea of being asked to make one. They were good friends and spoke and argued at first as such, but soon they both got very angry and excited, and McLaughlin, having a whip in his hand, forgot himself, and actually struck the other more than once with it, and then told him he was ready to give him any satisfaction he required. Dr. McDermot then left him, and McLaughlin came to me and told me the whole story, and that he, of course, expected a challenge at once, and begged I would go out with him, as his friend.

I was then lying in bed, far from well, but I consented on the understanding that he would allow me to use my own discretion in all and every way. While we were talking, the hostile message was brought by an officer, an Irishman, whom I found very stubborn and unreasonable then and afterwards; we talked over the affair, and I used my best endeavours to try and bring the matter to an amicable conclusion, admitting that my friend had committed himself most seriously, and was truly sorry for what he had done, and was ready and anxious to make the most ample apology; but the Irishman would not hear of anything less than a meeting, and said that nothing less would satisfy his friend or himself. It was finally settled that they should meet at a given place next morning, and with this understanding the obstinate Irishman left me. I now sent for McLaughlin and told him all that had passed, and that he must be prepared to go with me at the appointed hour next morning. He was quite cool and collected, and then left me, as he said, to arrange his papers and settle his affairs. He afterwards told me he was so employed during the best part of the night, and he also gave me certain instructions in case of anything happening to him. We kept our engagement punctually, and we found the others waiting for us with a medical man in attendance. After some talk and a toss up, it fell to my lot to measure the ground (twelve paces), to see the principals into their places, and to give the word or signal to fire; but I had previously told

McLaughlin to allow McDermot to fire first, then to fire his own pistol in the air, thus showing he had given his adversary the chance to shoot him, and by this action admitting himself to be in the wrong; all this my friend agreed to, and promised to do.

When they had taken their places I asked, "Are you ready?" and on being answered "Yes," I said, "Present," and so kept them for a few seconds, when I dropped my handkerchief as the signal to fire. McDermot fired and missed my friend, who instantly afterwards fired his pistol in the air. I stepped forward to McDermot's friend and said, "Gentlemen, I hope you are satisfied?" The Irishman answered, "Certainly not, they must go on." I endeavoured in vain to convince him that the rules of honour were satisfied, that his friend had had the chance of shooting mine, and that mine had fully acknowledged himself in the wrong by firing his pistol in the air. Dr. McDermot appeared to agree with me, but said he must leave all to his second; but the Irishman became more and more excited, and said he could not be satisfied until they had another shot or two. I then said, "Well, sir, it must be you and I to go on, for I cannot suffer these gentlemen to go any further; so come on." This worked a marvellous change, and my brave Irish boy soon became cool and reasonable; finally, we all shook hands and returned to Lisbon, and had a comfortable breakfast together in a café. This was the first and only duel I ever was concerned in, and yet in my early days duels and hard drinking were frequent evils, and considered by many to be both necessary and unavoidable.

CHAPTER XV

CHASED BY A PIRATE

Appointed captain in the 50th Regiment—Embark for Jamaica—A terrible storm and a drunken captain—Return to port—Sail again with another captain—Ship chased by a pirate—Jamaica once more

IN April, 1821, I again attended the Commander-in-Chief's Military Secretary's levée. Sir Henry Torrens was still in office, and when I told him of my anxiety to be employed he asked me where I would like to serve. I said, "Jamaica above all other parts of the world"; he then directed me to write to him to that effect. I did so next day, and three weeks afterwards had the pleasure of seeing myself appointed captain of a company in the 50th Regiment, and I soon received an official letter advising me to join the depot of the regiment in the Isle of Wight, which I did in the month of July following. I remained doing duty there for nearly twelve months, and it was during that period that I had a severe attack of inflammation of the eyes, which induced me to appeal to Lord Palmerston for the second, and last time, for my pension. We embarked for Jamaica in the hired ship *Echo*, but were detained by contrary winds in Cowes harbour for a fortnight. The captain had his wife on board during our detention, and we were so much pleased with his manner and polite attentions that we invited him to become our guest during the voyage (for in those days officers so embarked provided their own messing), and all went on well until a fine fair wind enabled us to sail: the captain then landed his wife, and from that hour and for ten days after he was never sober.

During this time the mate took charge, but in a few days we were met by a fearful gale right against us, and every hour and day it became worse and worse. Our captain still remained beastly drunk and most troublesome, every now and then throwing handfuls of silver, and some gold, amongst the soldiers on deck, allowing them to scramble for it, and when spoken to by any of us, swearing and damning and calling out that we were all going to Davy Jones's locker together.

The gale at last increased to a hurricane; the captain then became so troublesome that the senior officers present (Captain Powell and I) went officially to our commanding officer, Colonel P——, and advised him to confine the captain to his cabin, and to order the mate to take the ship back to port, as the sailors were already done up and grumbling. Colonel P—— was a good and kind man, but without energy or resolution, and he declined to interfere or to take any such responsibility on himself. We urged and urged our request, as the lives of all were in danger, but still finding Colonel P—— would not do anything, we insisted on having his leave to act, so that we might ourselves carry out his orders. He then said, " Well, boys, just do as you like." We then at once forced the captain off the deck into his cabin, and told him he must consider himself under arrest. He got very violent, and swore he would not be kept a prisoner by any one. Then we got him down again and placed two sentries in his cabin, with orders not to suffer him to go on deck. We next went to the mate and told him that his captain was a prisoner for habitual drunkenness and neglect of duty, and that he (the mate) should at once take the ship into port. This the honest sailor refused to do; he could not, he said, act without his captain's orders, that he would be dismissed by the owners and ruined if he did so. We reported accordingly to Colonel P——, who at once declined further responsibility. The gale continued without any visible change; many of our sails were blown away, the weather became very thick and dirty, our sailors were done up and discontented to a man, yet the mate would do nothing. He confessed the crew were overworked, but that he could not help it, and dared not go back. In this state we got through another day and night, and next morning found ourselves at daylight all but on shore on the island of Alderney, with only enough sea room to clear the rocks ahead of us, on which we must have been wrecked, had not the morning's dawn happily come in time to save us.

When clear in the open sea, we again urged the mate to bear away for the nearest harbour, but he still refused, urging his former reasons. We then begged him to parade the whole crew on the quarter-deck, that we might know their opinions. This he did, and the gallant fellows to a man declared they could not possibly work any longer, and urged us, for the safety of all, to put up in some harbour. For days we had made no observations, but being satisfied it was the island of Alderney we saw that morning the mate had no doubt of our whereabouts. We now went to Colonel P—— (who seldom left his cabin, for he had his wife and a young lady, Miss C——, with him), and we urged or rather insisted upon his signing a written order which we had prepared, directing the mate at once to take the ship back to the nearest port, telling Colonel P—— at the same time the danger we had escaped, and the result of our parade of the crew. As before, he resisted for some time all responsibility, but at last we got him to sign the order. Then followed difficulties with the mate, and it was not until we threatened to put a sentry over him that he consented, and gave the order to bear away and steer for Torbay. At four on the same evening land was reported ahead, and by sunset we were close in, and hoisted a signal of distress, which soon brought us a pilot boat, which boarded us and at once took us safely to anchor, thankful for our escape from destruction.

I now recommended Colonel P—— to report all that had occurred to us to the different authorities in London, and to state the necessity which obliged him to take all the responsibility and to act as he did. Poor man! he became more than ever confused, and said that he would be ruined and brought to a court-martial. I tried all I could to convince him, and he asked me to write the reports in his name, and said that he would sign them if I did so. I dispatched them at once, for fear of his altering his mind, and he soon received an answer approving of all he had done, and thanking him for his most able and judicious conduct.

On the same day the owners came down from London, bringing another captain with them. It was then found that the ship had suffered much, and carpenters and shipwrights were sent from the dockyard at Plymouth to examine and repair her. The owners were so pleased with the assistance which the soldiers gave the sailors during the gale, that they made the former a present of two tons of potatoes. It took more than a fortnight before the *Echo* was again reported fit for sea. During that time we amused ourselves landing and making excursions daily to different parts of the country, and in this interval Colonel P—— had a second letter, saying that our application for additional allowances for our losses during the storm was under favourable consideration; this enabled us to replenish our sea-stock, and to make due provision for our future comfort. We sailed again with a fair breeze, and in due course reached Madeira, where we remained for some days, landing frequently and enjoying ourselves much in that gay town.

From Madeira we soon got into the trade winds, and had delightful sailing, without any extraordinary occurrence, till we got off the island of St. Christopher, when one morning the captain came and roused us all from our beds, saying we were being chased by a pirate. This was startling news, for we had heard that these seas were full of pirates, and that they seldom showed mercy to any one. Our ladies and soldiers' wives began crying and moaning at once, for they expected nothing less than our utter destruction. Most of us hurried on deck in our night-dresses, and there saw a clipper brig bearing down upon us under all sail, about fifteen miles distant. Our captain still trusted that she might be a man-of-war, but when she fired a gun there was no doubt of her being a pirate. We returned in great excitement to our cabins and dressed with all dispatch. I then, as the next senior officer, went to Colonel P—— to report our situation, and to request his orders as to what we ought to do, and begged him to come up at once. His wife got alarmed, and he merely said he could do nothing; but at last told me, "Just do as you like." I returned on deck and consulted with the captain, who observed that it was useless to attempt to run away, as the stranger was gaining fast upon us, and had fired another gun to bring us to. Although we had about ten officers on board and about two hundred soldiers, all these were recruits, and we had not one stand of arms belonging to the troops nor to the ship. However, we decided to make some appearance, and ordered the soldiers to dress in their red coats and caps, to remain ready below, but not to move, till ordered on deck. Meantime the captain furled every sail, except his three top-sails, and with these and his colours flying he continued running easily before the wind. We could clearly see with our glasses the well-known pirates' flag, blue with a white death's-head, flying from the fore top-mast head and the decks crowded with men. Captain Fraser determined to continue our course till the pirate was all but on board of us, then to bring our ship sharp round to the wind, and our men to run up and show themselves in line under our bulwarks, with the officers flourishing their swords, to show we were all ready for action, expecting by this sudden manœuvre that the pirate would be right aboard or alongside of us before he had time to take in his crowd of sails, and, if so, that we might then have a chance of grappling and boarding him, when our numbers might give us some advantage; but we were no sooner round and brought to the wind than our adversary, as if by magic, had all his extra sails down, and was round to the wind as soon as we were, showing a splendid broadside of nine guns and a crew of no less than eighty men.

We were now within a few hundred yards of each other, and expected every minute a shot amongst us. Nothing was done for about ten minutes; the pirate then lowered his boat, and sent her fully manned to board us. Our captain said she must come to our leeside, and that our only chance was to secure them. This we agreed to do, and at once to dress one of their men in one of our sailor's clothes and to hang him up at our peak, so as to make the pirate believe that his men had taken possession of our ship. This was a desperate resolution, but as we expected no quarter from them we had no choice but to make the most of our perilous situation. Just as the boat came under our stern a signal of recall was made from the pirate, and the boat at once returned to the brig. We continued to look with additional anxiety, expecting every moment to see the boat come back, but for another ten minutes nothing was done, and our captain then ordered our ship to bear away and continue our course, so as to see what the pirate would do, and whether he would fire and bring us up again. But he thought better of it and allowed us to continue our course in peace, seeing no doubt that we were only troops and that he could not expect much booty from us. During the whole of this time Colonel P—— never left his cabin. His wife was crying and sobbing the whole time, and all his endeavours were to comfort her. Of the officers then present, only General Gallaway and myself are now living, and on that occasion Gallaway proved himself to be a promising young soldier, for he volunteered to lead the first boarders, should we succeed in grappling with the pirate.

We reached Port Royal in Jamaica a week afterwards, and at once reported our adventures to the admiral, Sir Edward Owen, and from the description our captain gave of the pirate our naval officers knew him well, and had often given him chase in vain. Two or three men-of-war were now sent to look for him, but returned in a few days without seeing him. Dozens of pirates, of various classes, were at this time cruising in these seas, and had made many captures, plundering and burning their prizes, and barbarously ill-treating and murdering their victims. We had a large naval force on the Jamaica station at this time, and they captured many of these lawless pirates, who were at once tried, and in every instance found guilty and sentenced to be hanged. I attended some of the trials and saw many of these daring fellows, who were plucky to the last, for they did not deny but actually gloried in their calling. They were men of all nations, but principally Italians and Spaniards. We landed on the following day at Kingston, and our different detachments of officers and men joined their respective regiments, viz., the 33rd, 50th, and 92nd.

The English mail which left England after us arrived at Port Royal some time before we did, and Colonel P—— found a letter waiting for him from the Secretary of War authorizing him to draw £80 as compensation for lost sea-stock during the gale already recorded. He therefore called a meeting of the officers who arrived in the *Echo*, and on our assembling read the letter, and proposed dividing the money amongst us, claiming three shares for himself—that is, for himself, his wife, and Miss C——. I said, "No, colonel; you only subscribed one share of our additional expenses, and you may remember that when we agreed to purchase extra provisions at Torbay we, the officers, declined to allow Mrs. P—— or Miss C—— to contribute one shilling to that expense." On this he got very angry and said, "Well, Captain Anderson, I'll bring you to a court-martial for attempting to obtain money under false pretences." I answered, "Very well, sir; I believe you signed these letters." He was thus settled, and most completely put about, and then said, "By G——! I think you are right"; so ended our dispute, and the money was divided share and share alike to each of us.

CHAPTER XVI

LIFE IN JAMAICA

Appointed deputy judge-advocate—Sir John Keane—An interesting court-martial—Sent with a small detachment to Port Maria—Awful outbreak of yellow fever

MAJOR-GENERAL HENRY CONRAN commanded in Jamaica at this time, and the billet of deputy judge-advocate being vacant by the death of Captain Tonge, the general, knowing that I had formerly held this position, at once appointed me to the office. This gave me additional work, and considerable increase of pay. About a year afterwards Major-General Sir John Keane succeeded General Conran, and he retained me still in the appointment. As he was a most uncertain man, my work was trebled, for he never hesitated to bring officers and men to court-martial, even for the most trifling offences. Here, in justice to myself, I must notice that I often told him so, but all to no purpose, for he was always obstinate, and would have his own way. I may give one instance. Some officers of the

90th had met together one evening in one of the rooms, and two of them got into an altercation, followed by strong and improper language, which induced the senior officers present to place them both under arrest and to report them next morning to their commanding officer, Major Charlton. He ordered a court of inquiry at once before himself in the messroom. Among the witnesses then examined was the paymaster, Captain Micklejohn, a truly noble fellow, who stated all he could remember of what took place on the previous night between the offending officers. He then left the room, but on getting outside and talking to some other officers (who were waiting to be examined) and stating the substance of his evidence to Major Charlton, one of them remarked, "But did you say so and so?" "Oh no, I entirely forgot that, but I shall instantly go back and state it." Micklejohn then begged to be allowed to add to his former evidence, but his commanding officer would not hear him, and desired him to retire. The offending officers, Major W—— and Ensign P——, were brought to general court-martial, and both were found guilty and sentenced to be cashiered. The sentences were approved by his Majesty, but in consideration of former services and the recommendation of the court they were ordered to be severely reprimanded and to return to their duty.

My reason for writing all this is that before

the same general court-martial Paymaster Micklejohn was arraigned for conduct unbecoming an officer and a gentleman, in withholding, at a court of inquiry by his commanding officer, evidence which he afterwards gave on oath before a general court-martial. I was the judge-advocate on these trials, and I used every endeavour and argument to convince Sir John Keane and Major Charlton of the injustice and cruelty of bringing an officer, and one of known character, to public trial on such charges, especially as he had returned voluntarily to his commanding officer at once, to offer the evidence which he had forgotten at the moment, thus proving that he did not willingly nor with any intention of screening the offenders withhold his evidence in the first instance. I also pressed upon them the difficulty, nay, the impossibility, for them to repeat word for word the conversation during our own interview; but all was to no purpose: they would not listen to reason, and so they determined he must be tried, and exposed to all the disgrace and annoyances of a general court-martial. He was tried, and the inquiry clearly showed that he did give evidence on oath before a general court-martial which he did not give at the court of inquiry. But it was distinctly proved that he did willingly, and at once, return with a free offer of that evidence, which was declined by his commanding officer. The court therefore found him guilty of not giving the full evidence before the court of inquiry which he gave before the general court-martial, but, under the circumstances which were so clearly shown as to the cause of the omission, the court acquitted the prisoner of all blame, though he was to be slightly reprimanded. This was no more than we all expected, and I told Sir John Keane before the trial that this and this only could be the end of it. I could name other instances equally frivolous and provoking; it is sufficient to say that very many others suffered through him in much the same way.

For the first two years of this my second visit to Jamaica I enjoyed very good health, and yet we had a considerable amount of sickness amongst the troops generally, and several of my friends of the good ship *Echo* died. As far as keeping away from the influence of the sun and living very temperately, of course I took every care of myself. Towards the close of the second year the negroes got very troublesome and insolent to their masters on the north side of the island, and on one or two occasions attempted to commit murder at a station called Port Maria. A company was generally, and for years, stationed at this place, but in consequence of the unusual mortality amongst the troops they were for some months withdrawn, and the barracks were deserted and allowed to fall into decay. During the above troubles the proprietors and inhabitants of Port

Maria made repeated applications to the governor, the Duke of Manchester, for a detachment, and his Grace referred their application to Sir John Keane; but the latter resisted on the plea that the station was considered by the chief medical officers so unhealthy as to be totally unfit for European soldiers, and, in proof of this, repeated how constant and great was the mortality on every former occasion when troops were stationed there. The inhabitants then said that the sickness and deaths which had taken place were all owing to the men being allowed to wander about the country and to get drunk at all hours. These statements and appeals were at last listened to by Sir John Keane, and he ordered a captain, two subalterns, and fifty picked, sober men from my regiment to be at once embarked for Port Maria, with a medical officer. This order was instantly carried out, and I was the unfortunate captain named for this duty. The morning for our embarkation I was sent for by Sir John Keane, who gave me the most strict orders about keeping my men constantly employed by drills and marching out in the mornings, and in the barracks during the days as much as possible, and above all I was to keep them away from all chances and temptations of drinking. He impressed upon me that I could have no excuse for intemperance or irregularities, as all my men were picked and sober soldiers from the different companies of the regiment. He desired me further to report to him by every day's post the state and health of my detachment.

All the previous reports we heard of this place damped our courage from the first, and both officers and men considered our present duties and chances very much like those of a forlorn hope; but on finding our barracks newly done up and painted, and in every way most comfortable, our fears almost vanished, and every succeeding day for a fortnight found us all more and more contented, so much so that we began to wish we might be allowed to remain there as long as we were to serve in Jamaica. In this mind and spirit I continued my daily reports to Sir John Keane, showing that we had not a man in hospital, and the men and officers were most happy and contented. We really were so, though our only society was the Rev. Mr. M—— and his family. With him I spent many happy hours, for I soon discovered that during the Peninsular War he was one of the Duke of Wellington's principal spies, with the rank of captain in the army, although he never joined a regiment in his life. He was by birth a German, spoke many languages, and was a most intelligent man and a good and sincere Christian. It was very difficult to make him speak of his former exploits, but when he did he told us wonderful tales of several marvellous hairbreadth

LIFE IN JAMAICA 129

escapes in all kinds of characters and disguises, and I know from all reports that he was one of the most efficient and successful spies. After the Peace of 1815 many half-pay officers studied for the Church and took holy orders, and this reverend gentleman was amongst the number.

Up to this time the weather was dry and beautiful, but heavy rains then followed, and continued for a week or more. Our barracks were situated on a high neck of land projecting some distance into the sea, and on our right there was a large mangrove swamp, almost dry until the rains commenced. Then, filling from the hills and valleys to overflowing, it suddenly burst towards the sea, carrying all before it, and from that hour the stench became so powerful that we were all obliged to keep our handkerchiefs to our noses, and so save ourselves as much as possible from its fearful and disgusting effects. From the very first hour of this escape of water, mud, and decayed vegetable matter the whole air became actually poisonous, and our poor men fell sick daily, and in most cases they died before the following day. Some were carried off a few hours after they were attacked, amongst these my own servant, who attended us in good health at breakfast and was dead and buried at night.

I continued well and able to attend to my duties, and by each post reported our sufferings and losses to the Commander-in-Chief. Then, after losing nearly half of my detachment, I received an order to hold all in readiness to embark on the shortest notice to return to headquarters at Kingston, leaving such sick men as could not be removed in charge of our medical officer. This good news I made known at once, and it was received with three cheers. Next morning a smart clipper was seen standing in for our anchorage, and I instantly sent one of my officers down to the landing-place with instructions to wave his hat as soon as a boat came on shore, if he heard the vessel was for us. We watched him with all eyes and the deepest anxiety, and as the boat landed up went his hat; three loud cheers followed from us, and I at once gave orders for immediate parade and embarkation. In half an hour all who could move were on parade and with our baggage packed ready to move off. On wheeling the detachment back into sections and giving the words "Quick march!" agonizing cries and screams (which I can never forget) were faintly heard from the few poor sick men who were left behind in hospital. There were seven of these unfortunates, and all urged the doctor to allow them to go with the others, saying they would run all risks and would prefer death before reaching the beach, rather than be deserted and left to die there; but the medical officer saw they were too weak to be removed, and tried to comfort them by saying that he himself ran the same risk by remaining with them. We left them, indeed, with great sorrow, and in less than an hour we were safely embarked on board the *Mandeville* and off for Port Royal. Our happy escape from Port Maria, the change of scene and air, soon restored our men to their usual health; but it was very different with the poor fellows left behind, for we heard that three of the number soon died; the remaining four joined us later. I afterwards heard that the barracks at Port Maria were burnt and levelled to the ground by the Government.

CHAPTER XVII

HOME AGAIN AND MARRIED

Invalided to England—Ship injured on coral rock—Dangerous voyage—Married on 25th November, 1826—Portsmouth—The Duke of Clarence—Ireland—Complimented by Sir Hussey Vivian on execution of difficult manœuvres

I REMAINED doing duty in Jamaica for some weeks longer, but began to get anxious to get home, and latterly my health became indifferent. In February, 1825, I applied for a medical board, which recommended me for a year's leave of absence, and with this prospect my health began to improve. The Government decided to send home a number of invalid soldiers, and I was commanded to take charge of them. I was not sorry, for by this chance I was allowed a free passage home. There were several other officers who were also going home on sick leave in the *Speake*. In all there were about two hundred men, a few women and children, and an assistant-surgeon.

We sailed on the 6th of March, and all went

well till the night of the 9th, when, with a beautiful clear moon shining, we suddenly ran aground on the outer coral rock of the small and low island of Magna. Fortunately the night was calm, so that we were running not more than three or four miles an hour. The full moon gave us nearly the light of day, and before sunrise we could see the island low but distinctly above the horizon, and then our captain changed our course to steer clear of the land, but the currents must have got hold of us; yet it seemed to me the captain and his chief officer were much to blame, for they were both actually walking the deck when she struck, and had been there for hours before in a clear night. Had there been a proper look out no such accident ought to have taken place. We, the passengers, were all asleep at the time, but the sudden shock and bump of striking roused us all instantly. Officers, soldiers, and women rushed at once without dressing on deck, where the confusion and screaming for some minutes became fearful; but the captain and agent assured us that there was land in front of us and that come what may we need not be alarmed for our lives, as we could all be landed with safety. Meanwhile two of the boats were lowered and carried our anchors astern, and with hawsers from these we tried to work the ship off the rocks into deep water, and my endeavours were equally pressing to clear the decks and to get all who were not wanted for work to go below. It was not till I went down with them and pledged my word to all that I should not leave the ship until the very last man of my charge was landed that I got them all to obey me.

Order was then so far restored, and from over the ship's side we could distinctly see the coral rocks upon which we were fixed, and soon afterwards, from the violent bumping, parts of our copper and sheathing got detached. The low, sandy island, without tree or other vegetation, was within a few hundred yards of us, and every possible effort was continued to heave her off, but all to no purpose. The boats and anchors were then moved first off one quarter and then off the other, and in each of these positions the heavy pulls and straining moved her head and stern round a little. It was then clearly shown that she was fixed as on a pivot in the centre, from which no efforts could move her. The pumps were then tried, and she was found to be making a little water, but not sufficient to cause any unnecessary alarm. At the critical moment it was ascertained that the tide must soon flow inwards, and as both crew and troops were fairly done up it was determined to wait patiently for the tide, when, if the ship made no water, she would be sure to float off. Meantime preparations were made for landing a quantity of provisions and water in case of necessity, and the officers and men packed their portmanteaux and knapsacks

HOME AGAIN AND MARRIED

ready to make the best of the island of Magna if obliged to land there. About four in the morning the tide began to make, and by six the good ship was afloat again. She was then towed by the boats into deep water and the anchors let go, the pumps tried, and a strict examination made into our condition, when it was found that the leak and water had increased. For some time the captain and agent were undecided whether to continue the voyage or to return to Port Royal, but after waiting for a couple of hours they determined to pass a sail under the ship's bottom and haul it as tight as it could be made, and then to continue the voyage to England. This was done, and we were again steering our way with a fair wind and fine weather. It was well for us that our vessel was built of teak, which enabled her to stand the bumping and thumping, which would at once destroy most ships. We now had New Providence Island before us in our course, in case of being obliged to seek shelter, but all went well till we got off Bermuda, when we were overtaken by a strong gale and heavy sea. The ship laboured much, and the men at the pumps discovered that the water had increased, but as the wind was off the land we had no choice but to run on for England. The pumps kept going during the days and nights. Our commander and our agent showed the best example by their constant watching and exertions; we soon began to lose all our fears in the sure hope of a speedy voyage and a happy end to our troubles, and in another fortnight we were safely anchored at Spithead.

Our arrival was reported to the authorities in London, and orders came down directing us to proceed without delay to Sheerness. I got leave to land and go to London, on the understanding that I should on the following day go to Sheerness, there to await the arrival of my charge and proceed with them to Fort Pitt, Chatham, and so to deliver them, and their accounts, to the authorities at that station. I applied to General Thornton for leave of absence, but this was flatly refused, until he was satisfied and could report favourably on the state of my depot. Soon afterwards I had the chance of repeating verbally my desire for leave of absence, but as usual he refused, saying it would be a pity to leave my depot for some time longer, as they were getting on so well. I then told him frankly that I was engaged to be married for some time past; that he had obliged me twice already to put it off, and to break my word and my faith; that if he did so any longer my character and my honour must suffer. On this he laughed heartily and said, "This alters matters; of course, you must go immediately. Send me your application, but you need not wait for an answer—you may start at once." By that night's post I wrote to my beloved one, told her my difficulties were passed, and that I hoped to be with her soon after she received my letter, and that she alone could now complete my happiness. Three days more found me in London, received with open arms, and lodged in Park Street. A fortnight was allowed to make the necessary dresses and preparations, then my happiness was made perfect. I was married on the 25th November, 1826, at St. Pancras Church, London, to Miss Mary Campbell, only daughter of Colonel Alexander Campbell, by the Rev. Joseph Brakenbury.

In the August following his Royal Highness the Duke of Clarence, as Lord High Admiral of England, visited Portsmouth and honoured the 50th Regiment by presenting us (on Southsea Common, in presence of all the troops in garrison) with new colours, accompanied by a most flattering speech. After the review his Royal Highness, the Duchess of Clarence, and the Colonel-in-Chief, General Sir James Duff, and many of the county families of Hampshire, were entertained at a luncheon in Portsmouth by the officers of the regiment. Lady Duff and my dear wife had the honour of receiving our guests, and about three hundred sat down.

I must here mention a remarkable instance of his Royal Highness's memory. On his arrival at Portsmouth I was introduced to him by General Sir James Lyons, commanding the garrison, and on mentioning our wish that he should do us the honour to present our new colours he said, "Yes, I shall be very happy; I know the history of your regiment quite well, but you may bring me a memorandum on a card of the different actions it has been in." Next morning I returned to his Royal Highness with a neatly written card showing the battles in which the regiment had been engaged, commencing with Minden, August, 1759. Looking at it, he said, "Sir, you had not a man at Minden; your regiment was then quartered at Haslar barracks." I answered, "I beg your Royal Highness's pardon, but we always thought our regiment, or some portion of it, was at Minden, and I have myself seen an old breast-plate with the word 'Minden' on it, but I will have another card made out and omit the word." "Quite unnecessary," he said, and, taking his pen, he scratched it out. I then observed that a very old gentleman who was once in the regiment was then living near Portsmouth, and that I would go and see him, as he might perhaps give me some information on the subject. I took my leave and returned to barracks, and told my colonel and the other officers about my conversation with his Royal Highness; they all laughed, and maintained that our flank companies were at Minden, and urged me to go at once and see old Captain Thompson. I found him, and he in like manner maintained that our flank companies were at Minden. I returned in triumph, fully believing that his Royal Highness was wrong, and on waiting on him next day I mentioned my interview with Captain Thompson; but again he said, "No, no; you had not a man there," so I took my leave to prepare for the morrow's parade. We decided on writing to the Army Agents, Messrs. Cox & Co., begging them to go at once to the War Office and request an immediate inspection of the public returns of that period, and of the troops employed at the battle of Minden. In due course we received their answer stating that we had not a man of the 50th Regiment there. His Royal Highness remained at Portsmouth ten days longer, and was entertained daily during that time.

We embarked in a steamer at Liverpool on the 29th June, 1830, and landed on the following forenoon at Dublin. Next morning the 50th Regiment marched in two divisions, headquarters and six companies, under Colonel Woodhouse, for Waterford, and four companies under my command to Clonmel, and in a few months we moved on to Templemore, with detachments at Thurles and Roscrea; and here we enjoyed ourselves very much, Sir Henry Garden and other residents in the neighbourhood having shown us every attention. I was for some time in command of the regiment at Templemore, and it was here that I first had the honour of forming the acquaintance of Lieut.-

General Sir Hussey Vivian (afterwards Lord Vivian), who then came to us on a tour of inspection, and who expressed himself much pleased with the regiment. He was very fond of introducing field movements of his own, and on this occasion asked me to "change front from open column to the rear on a centre company." I told him there was no such movement in the book—but that I would at once do it. He said, "Stop, until I explain it to you." I begged he would not, but allow me to proceed, and without hesitation I ordered the right centre company to wheel on its centre to the rear, the left wing to go to the right about, and then ordering the right centre company to stand fast, and all the others to form line on that company, by right shoulders forward, the left wing halting and fronting by companies, as they got into the new line, followed by independent file firing from the centre, and by each company as they got into the new alignments, supposing this sudden change of front to be occasioned by the unexpected appearance of an enemy from a wood in our former rear. This fire was kept up for some time, and then we charged the supposed enemy and carried all before us.

Sir Hussey was much pleased, and when our manœuvring was over he ordered me to form the regiment into hollow square, and then addressed us, and complimented me very much, saying I was the first commanding officer who at once took up his ideas of providing against a sudden surprise from an enemy, and that he "should not fail to make a special report of my efficiency." And I know that afterwards he did so, and that when he got next day to Birr barracks, to inspect the 59th Regiment, he called upon the colonel of that regiment to do the same manœuvre, in which that officer altogether failed, and then Sir Hussey again spoke of how "Major Anderson and the 50th had performed his wishes without the slightest hint or hesitation." I have mentioned this at length, because it was much talked of at the time, and I was really proud of the opinion of so able and distinguished an officer, and because, as I shall hereafter show, this trifle led to much good to me some years afterwards.

CHAPTER XVIII

TO NEW SOUTH WALES

Dr. Doyle's sermon—Ordered to New South Wales—Sail for Sydney with three hundred convicts—Mutiny at Norfolk Island—Appointed colonel commandant there

I WAS detached with four companies to Maryborough : soon afterwards the well-known priest, the Rev. Dr. Doyle, visited the place, and on the Saturday of his arrival it was publicly announced that he would preach in the Catholic chapel. Being a very celebrated and popular preacher, many of the Protestant inhabitants attended ; the church was crowded beyond comfort and standing-room, and all waited past the appointed hour with anxiety and impatience. At last he appeared in front of the altar in his full white robes, and, fronting the congregation, stared fiercely and wildly all around the assembled crowd ; he then took off his biretta and threw it violently at his feet, and with his right arm stretched out and his fist clenched he shouted : " I have not come to preach to you, you midnight assassins, you skull-crackers! I am come to tell you that the hand of God is suspended over you, and that you shall not know the end thereof, until you are swept from the face of this earth and open your eyes in hell!"

The congregation moaned and crossed themselves again and again; there followed endless sobs and lamentation, then a dead silence for a minute or two. The Rev. Father now roused himself again and said (pointing to me), "There is the officer commanding the troops, he has got the King's commission in his pocket; and" (turning round to another part of the gallery) "there is the officer commanding the police, he has got the Lord-Lieutenant's commission in his pocket; and I have got" (slapping his hand violently on his side) "the seal of Christ in my pocket. You midnight assassins, go and repent of your sins, while you have yet time." He then retired, and the congregation broke up moaning and crossing themselves as before, and my dear wife and I were truly glad to escape without further fear of molestation. The cholera was raging at this time, and such was the terror occasioned amongst the lower classes by the Rev. Father's denunciation that it was said the deaths from cholera were more than usual for some time afterwards.

We returned to Birr barracks after this, leaving a strong detachment still at Maryborough, and early in April a letter was received by our commanding officer to hold the regiment in readiness to embark for New South Wales. The ship *Parmelia* took on board some of her freight of convicts at Gravesend, then sailed for the Cove of Cork to embark the remainder; there we received two hundred more, making in all about three hundred criminals. They were under the medical charge of Dr. Donoughoe, a very pleasing Irishman, and our captain during the voyage was equally pleasant. We were detained some weeks at the Cove from adverse winds and other causes, and during that time it was very distressing to witness the daily scenes which took place between the Irish convicts and their numerous heart-broken relations. They came in boatloads to our ship daily; they were not allowed to come on board, but only to talk to their kindred, who crowded over the ship's side or at the port-holes, and these interviews lasted for hours. At last, about the beginning of November, 1833, we got clear off and sailed for Sydney. The voyage was long, but on the whole pleasant. The convicts behaved well except on one occasion, when one nearly murdered another by striking him violently on the head with a pumice stone used for scrubbing the decks. For this daring and murderous assault the offender was placed in heavy irons, and next morning the whole of the convicts were paraded on deck, and with my detachment under arms and loaded, on the poop and in the cuddy, the prisoner was brought forward, stripped, and tied to the main rigging, and there received the severe corporal punishment of a hundred lashes. This had the desired effect, and from that day all was order and regularity. We arrived in Sydney on the 2nd March, 1834; the convicts were landed next day and marched to their quarters, and my detachment to the Sydney barracks.

I brought letters of introduction to the governor, General Sir Richard Bourke, from Sir Hussey Vivian, and also from Lord Stanley, then Secretary for the Colonies. With these I called at Government House; but the governor was at that time engaged and could not see me, so I left my letters with the aide-de-camp, who requested me to call next morning. Meanwhile Sydney was in a great state of excitement in consequence of news having just been received of a general mutiny of the prisoners at Norfolk Island, and an attack upon the troops there, with the loss of several lives. This mutiny had occupied the minds of the prisoners for many months, and was so planned that they were to attack the guards in gangs simultaneously, armed with hatchets, hoes, crowbars, and hammers, on going forth from their prisons to work; they were then to bind their victims and keep them in front, as shields, while others, with the captured arms, attacked the main body of the troops in barracks.

They had arranged to treat the free population with barbarity and cruelty too fearful to mention, and to quarter the colonel and the captain alive. I may mention that it came out in evidence during the trials that more than half the prisoners were for weeks consulting and planning the best modes of attack and of securing their purpose, and settling what to do afterwards, if successful. Their final decision was that an unusually large number should sham illness on the morning fixed for the attack, and so go (as usual each morning) to the hospital, and there secure the doctor and all the attendants, and then wait ready to make a rush behind a corner of the gaol, where a sergeant's guard of twelve men from the garrison attended daily to receive and to take charge for the day of the gaol-gang—amounting generally to thirty or forty of the very worst convicts in double heavy irons. After this they intended to escape from the island by the next Government vessel arriving. There were at this time only a hundred soldiers with a captain and two subalterns of the 4th Regiment on the island, and the prisoners amounted to seventeen hundred of the most desperate culprits on the face of the earth, but happily they were completely defeated, with the loss of only a few lives.

I attended at Government House next morning as directed, and was kindly received by Sir Richard Bourke, and after asking me a few questions about our voyage he said, " You brought me some letters, Major Anderson, and I am told you would like to be actively employed. You have, of course, heard the news from Norfolk Island. I shall be happy to give you the command, if you like." I answered that I myself would much like the appointment, but that I was a married man, and feared my wife would not like going there, after all we had heard of the desperate state of the prisoners, but that if his Excellency would give me an hour to consult my wife I should then return to him with my answer. He said, " Certainly, I will give you till to-morrow morning to make up your mind." I hurried home and told my wife all, and said that I saw no risk in accepting so good an appointment; but she, under the alarm of all she had just read in the papers, said nothing could tempt her to go there. I almost despaired of getting her consent, till at last I proposed that I should submit to the consideration of Sir Richard Bourke that I would gladly accept the appointment, if he would kindly give me the option of giving it up at once, should my wife dislike to remain there. He received me kindly, heard my request, and said, " Certainly, I shall not keep you a day longer there than you wish; meantime, I am going to-morrow to my country house at Parramatta, and I shall be glad if you and Mrs. Anderson will spend a few days there with us, and we can talk the matter over." I thanked him for his kindness, and said we should be most happy to accept his invitation; I then returned to my wife much pleased, and next day we went to Government House, Parramatta, and were very kindly received by the governor and his daughter. We remained there three days, and his Excellency took much pains to persuade my wife that there was no danger in going to Norfolk Island, as we should always have a sufficient number of troops to ensure our safety, that the climate was the best in the world, and our accommodation very good, and far beyond anything we could desire or expect. On leaving, the governor desired me to come to him next day in Sydney, saying that I should then receive my final instructions. I did so, and was told to hold myself in readiness to embark in a few days, and that my first duty on arrival should be to take depositions against all the convicts who were implicated in the late mutiny, and to transmit the same to the Colonial Secretary for the decision of the Attorney-General. I was then sent to the court to be sworn in as a magistrate of the territory, and finally told that the Government schooner *Isabella* would be ready to receive me and my family in a few days, and to sail at once for Norfolk Island.

We embarked on the 12th March, 1834, for my important command. For the first two or three days we had pleasant weather, but then it blew hard, with the wind right against us, and was very boisterous for a week. Our provisions now became short, and from this and the severity of the weather we were very much inconvenienced, but at last had a favourable change and made Norfolk Island in safety, and fortunately on a fine calm day; for in bad weather the landing there is always dangerous. I was received on the beach by a guard of honour of the 4th Regiment and by Captain Foster-Fyans, who was then acting-commandant (Colonel Morrisett and his family having previously sailed to Sydney). Captain Fyans invited us all to his quarters to breakfast, and an excellent one we had; nor must I omit mentioning how our dear children enjoyed the abundance of cream and fruits set before them, after the hard biscuits and salt pork which was their only food on board.

After breakfast, Captain Fyans took us to Government House, with which we were much pleased. It was a substantial building of one story and standing conspicuously by itself, on high ground; the rooms were numerous and well proportioned, the whole premises at the back being secured within a high wall and the windows in front by iron bars. Thus the whole residence might be considered (in case of an attack) a fortress; there were also in front of the house two eighteen-pounder guns mounted, and the military barracks were not a hundred yards distant. I may add the prisoners' gaols and other buildings were within a thousand yards, and the guns before the house commanded the whole. The more we saw the more we were delighted with our future quarters and prospects. By this time a considerable portion of our baggage had been landed and was arriving fast at Government House, and before night we were as well settled and comfortable as if we had been there for months.

CHAPTER XIX

NORFOLK ISLAND

Life at Norfolk Island—Trial of the mutineers—A fresh conspiracy—Execution of thirteen mutineers

NEXT day I assumed my duties, and proceeded at once to take depositions against the prisoners charged with the late mutiny. As is usually the case on such occasions, many of the convicts concerned turned King's evidence, and the most willing of all these informers was a desperate and cowardly villain named K——, who was at one time a captain in our navy, and after various crimes was at last transported for forgery. He had been many years a convict, and was always foremost in every crime which promised him a chance of escape, yet when detected always turned King's evidence; but still he was trusted by his companions on account of an extraordinary influence he had over them, and on this occasion chiefly because he was the only one of them who understood navigation, and could steer to a place of safety in the event of success in capturing the island and gaining the shipping. Of course he took the lead, and under his instructions the whole plan was for months secretly and most ably arranged; consequently his evidence, and that of many others whom he named, and who willingly came forward to save themselves, confirmed without doubt the guilt of all the leading conspirators, so that in a few days the depositions taken by me were complete against about fifty of the most daring characters. For six weeks all went peacefully, all the prisoners concerned being kept heavily ironed in gaol, awaiting the result.

In the meantime we continued making ourselves comfortable, daily visiting and exploring various parts of the island, and each day made us more happy in our lot. The island is evidently of volcanic origin, and abounds in valleys in every direction, and in each of these there is a stream of most pure crystal water. Lemons and citrons of the very best kinds grow everywhere, and are so common in every part of the island that many are allowed to drop from the trees and rot. Guavas and Cape gooseberries are equally common, and at one time oranges were in abundance; but my predecessor had all the trees destroyed, as affording too great a luxury to the prisoners! By convict labour excellent roads have been made everywhere. The climate is the best in the world, with always a bracing air, never too hot nor too cold. There were many hundreds of cattle and some thousands of Government sheep on the island, so that all the free population had a ration of fresh meat daily, and the officers were allowed to buy as much more as they wished, and flour also, at the commissariat, at a nominal price, never exceeding twopence the pound. All the officers had also gardens and convict servants to work them. All had likewise as many pigs and poultry as they chose to rear. My garden at Orange Vale was a splendid one, abounding with everything one could desire. We made about four hundred pounds of the best coffee annually, and many hundreds of pounds of arrowroot. My pigs and poultry were kept near Government House, together with dozens of turkeys, geese, guinea-fowls, and ducks. All our stock was fed from the refuse of the prisoners' breakfasts and from damaged corn, so that we incurred no expense by keeping such numbers. We made the best bacon that was ever known, and in large quantities, but could not succeed in making hams. When the convict servants failed in this, our medical men tried to secure success, but never succeeded; there was something in the air which caused them to decay. We had tradesmen and mechanics of every kind, and were allowed to have our boots and clothing of every description made for us. The woods of the island were very beautiful, and supplied material for handsome furniture of every kind.

All these advantages I had as commandant without any limits, but no officer could get anything done without a written requisition to me. The public dairy was near my house, and every officer, soldier, and free person on the island got a daily allowance of milk and butter. With all these advantages we lived most comfortably and almost for nothing.

The troops behaved remarkably well. We had only six court-martials during the whole period of my command. All the soldiers had gardens near their barracks, in which they grew all sorts of vegetables; they were also allowed to keep fowls. This not only kept them in excellent health, but gave them employment, and they were always at hand and ready for any emergency which might arise.

At last a ship was reported in sight, and proved to be his Majesty's ship *Alligator*, Captain Lambert, with Judge Burton and a military jury on board, for the trial of the mutineers. They were at once landed, the judge and some of the officers taking their quarters with me, the others with the officers of the garrison. Our carpenters were then set to work to prepare a spare room in the prisoners' barracks as a temporary court-house. This being soon completed, the trials commenced next day, and were continued day after day for a fortnight. Fifty of the leading conspirators were found guilty: more than half the number were sentenced to death, the others to transportation in irons for life. During the whole of this time the frigate was moored off the settlement, within easy range, in case of any fresh disturbance. Two days after the trials, Judge Burton spoke to me officially, and said he had the power of ordering some of the worst of the prisoners who were sentenced to death to be executed at once, before the frigate left, but that he would prefer not doing so till the Governor and Council saw the proceedings, provided I felt sure I could be answerable for their safe custody in the absence of the frigate. My answer was that I felt no fear about their safe custody, and had no hesitation in taking the responsibility; he then said, "We had better put all this in writing. I shall at once write to you on the subject, and let me have your answer as soon as possible." He did so, and in an hour had my answer. Judge Burton and the military jury sailed next day.

They had not been gone twenty hours before I received positive information through my police that another general mutiny was brewing, with the intention in the first instance to attack the gaol and release all the condemned prisoners. This was startling, but I decided to wait for further proofs. Next morning I had the names of about fifty of the new conspirators brought to me, and as most of them were well known to be desperate characters, I gave instant orders for their arrest. They were heavily ironed, and confined in different parts of the gaol, and, as I fully expected, two or three of them offered to give me evidence. I had them brought before me and examined, and each satisfied me that efforts were being made for a general rising to rescue the condemned, and that it was checked just in time, before more serious consequences could follow. I now told the informers that they must be sent back amongst the others, so as to deceive them, and make them feel sure that they had made no disclosures as to the guilt of their comrades, and that when all was over they would not be forgotten. Had I not done this, these men would have been marked afterwards by every convict on the island as informers, and would have been sure of vengeance in some way, sooner or later.

After these precautions all was peace for two months; then the Government brig *Governor Phillip* was reported. Our usual armed boat was sent off, and brought back as passengers the Rev. Mr. Styles, the Rev. Father McEncroe, and the hangman, and dispatches for me ordering the execution of thirteen of the most guilty of the mutineers. All the others were commuted to hard labour for life. It was left to my discretion to carry out these most distressing executions at such time and in such manner as I deemed safe, taking care that all prisoners on the island should be present, and that the condemned should have the presence and benefit of their respective clergymen for at least three days before the execution. I issued written orders proclaiming my warrant and authority for the execution, naming the unfortunates who were doomed to die, fixing two mornings for carrying out the sentences, and ordering one half of the convicts to be marched from their barracks and formed into close columns in front of the gaol, on the walls of which the gallows was erected, while the other half of the convicts could see from the barracks all that was going on. This was the order for the first day, when seven of the culprits suffered, and the remainder were disposed of in the same way the next morning. Before the execution I addressed the convicts, and said that if they attempted to move or to show any sign of resistance the officer in the stockade had my positive order to open fire on them at once. These preparations being all completed, the seven men were brought forward, dressed in white and attended by their clergy. They were composed and silent, and in a few seconds all was over. Not a word, not a murmur, escaped from the assembled mass. The following morning the same arrangements were made for the other half of the convicts to witness the execution of the remaining culprits, and all passed over as before. From that time order reigned on the island during the whole of my government, from March, 1834, to April, 1839.

CHAPTER XX

SUNDAY SERVICES AT NORFOLK ISLAND

I appoint two convicts (who had been educated for the Church) to officiate—Find about a hundred ex-soldiers among the convicts—Separate them from the others, with great success

THE Rev. Mr. Styles and Father McEncroe remained a fortnight with us, and took much pleasure in exploring the island. They left, promising to use their best endeavours to have clergymen sent to us, but none came for two years after this. On my arrival the only Sunday service we had for the prison population was more a mockery than a benefit. All the convicts, whether Protestants, Catholics, or Jews, were paraded together and marched up in single file to a field strongly fenced in, and there locked up. Then an officer stepped forward to the fence and there read the prayers and litany of the Church of England, not a word of which could be heard by the prisoners. They were then marched back to their prison yards, and there locked up for the

SUNDAY SERVICES 159

remainder of the day. The troops and free population had prayers read to them in the military barracks. I renewed my application for clergymen, but the answer invariably was that none could be found to take up the appointment.

This distressed me much, and, looking over the register of the convicts some time after this, I discovered that one of the number was transported for forgery while actually a chaplain on board an English man-of-war, and also that another had been educated as a Roman Catholic priest. These two men had behaved well since their arrival, so I thought it possible I might make something of them. I sent for Taylor and told him that I had discovered the cause and offence for which he had been sent there, and I was glad to hear he was now considered a steady man. I then spoke of the sad position of our convicts from their need of religious teaching, and said that I considered what was now being done a mere mockery, and that it was doing more harm than good; also that I knew what he had been, and what he could do if earnest and willing; that I would remove him from the other prisoners, give him a comfortable hut to live him, plain clothes, and a convict servant to attend him, and finally, if I saw hopes of doing any good, that I intended without delay to build a temporary church for him, and place there a pew for myself and my civil officers, that I might have the opportunity of hearing him occasionally and judging for myself. He was delighted and appeared most anxious and earnest. I dismissed him with the hope that he would seriously ponder over all I had said, and pray to God to assist him and to sanctify his endeavours.

I then sent for the other, and spoke in the same way to the same effect; he also most gladly and willingly entered into my wishes and promised much. That same evening I put them both in my written orders to be separated at once from their respective gangs, to be quartered by themselves, and to read the services of their respective Churches to the prisoners. This gave general satisfaction, and on the following Sunday the Protestants were separated from the Catholics, and each division marched to their respective places of worship, where the services were read to them for the first time. This was continued every succeeding Sunday with such success that pulpits, altars, and pews were soon built and forms provided sufficient for each congregation, and in due time I made it my duty to attend occasionally at either service, and I was always much pleased with the order and regularity which prevailed in both churches. The soldiers and free population continued their worship as usual at the barracks.

These arrangements succeeded so well that I reported the whole to the Government, and by return of mail I had the satisfaction to receive

SUNDAY SERVICES

the Governor's approval of all my proceedings and his desire that the same arrangements should be continued, as he could not then prevail on any clergyman to go to the island. In course of a few months I became quite convinced that our humble endeavours were doing much good, that our acting ministers were conducting themselves well, and that they were respected and looked up to by their former associates. I therefore made a report of this to the Government, and recommended that they should be further encouraged by a salary of one shilling a day and the promise of a commutation of their sentence hereafter, if recommended by me for continued good conduct. All this was granted, and I had much pleasure in promulgating the same and in carrying it all out.

For two years this went on with much success, and greatly to my satisfaction. Then we got into trouble. Two convicts attempted the lives of two of their comrades, on different occasions, without any previous cause of quarrel, and, as they afterwards admitted, for no other reason than that they were tired of their own lives and wished to get hanged! The first attack occurred when the convicts were going out from their barracks after breakfast to their daily work. This gang was going to farm labour, armed with field hoes. Without a word of previous warning the would-be assassin raised his hoe and with all his might struck the convict in front of him on the head, knocking him down insensible with a fearful wound in his skull. The unfortunate sufferer was at once taken to the hospital, and remained unconscious for many days. When he recovered he clearly proved that he had never had any previous quarrel, nor had he ever even spoken to the prisoner before. The other case was that of a convict who had got away from his gang and concealed himself in the hut of one of the overseers (who was allowed to live and remain there at night), and whom he had determined to murder. He hid himself behind the door, and when the overseer entered he knocked him down senseless, but happily two other men followed, who at once secured the culprit. These cases were too serious for me to deal with, so I took the necessary depositions and sent them on to the Colonial Secretary for the consideration of the Attorney-General, and by the next arrival of our ship Judge Plunket and a military jury came for the trial of these two men. They were found guilty and sentenced to be hanged; the execution took place a few days later, in the presence of all the convicts, without a murmur. One of the men who had been assaulted recovered in due time, but the other died, and from that day we never had another serious crime.

I discovered from the registers that I had about one hundred former soldiers (amongst the prison population of seventeen hundred) from regiments in India and the Australian colonies, all transported for assaulting or threatening the lives of their officers, generally while under the influence of drink. I ordered them to be all paraded for my inspection, and then said to them, "I find you have been soldiers. I know that you were sent here for assaulting, or threatening to shoot, your officers in your drunken bouts. I have examined your registers and know all about you. Now, I am a soldier, and consider you are still almost soldiers, so I shall at once separate you from your present associates, whose offences have been very different to yours. Most of them are criminals of the worst and deepest dye—murderers, thieves, and assassins. Their companionship must in time degrade you and make you desperate, and perhaps as bad as themselves. I shall therefore try to save you as far as I can. I shall place you in rooms and messes by yourselves, and in separate working gangs. More than this, if I require you I shall put arms in your hands; for you have been soldiers (as I am now), so I shall not be afraid to trust you if I require you!"

They began to cheer with delight, which I at once stopped, reminding them that I could not allow any such expression of their feelings, and that from them I must expect perfect discipline and quiet obedience; then I concluded by saying, "In this way I mean to trust you so long as you behave yourselves and deserve my support, but if I ever again, from this day, see you speak one word to, or associate in any way with, your former companions, back again you go to them, there to remain always as outcasts in misery." They were delighted, and could only with difficulty restrain expressions of their joy, and from that hour my arrangements were carried out admirably to the last. The mass of prisoners were, however, for some time, much annoyed by this arrangement and partiality; but after longer reflection, I was assured, they were glad of it, as it showed them that reason and justice ruled the commandant, and that belief caused a general disposition towards good order and regularity.

I may say that, taking them as a whole, and remembering their previous numerous and great crimes, the convicts during my superintendence behaved wonderfully well. After the capital crimes already mentioned we had but individual offences, such as striking or threatening their constables and overseers, disobedience of orders, and neglecting their work. For these misdeeds they were always sent to gaol, and brought before me in petty session next morning, and if found guilty, on sworn evidence, sentenced to a week or fortnight, a month or two months' imprisonment in irons in gaol, according to their offences. In more serious and aggravated cases they were sentenced to corporal punishment—from fifty or a hundred to three hundred lashes; but these instances were comparatively few, and always avoided if possible. The average of the latter punishments, in my time, was from seventy to seventy-five cases a year, whereas in Colonel Morrisett's time they always exceeded one thousand, though he had not at any time more than twelve hundred prisoners, while with me their number increased year by year, until we had over seventeen hundred.

CHAPTER XXI

LIFE AT NORFOLK ISLAND

Solitary case of misconduct among the soldier gang—I get many pardoned and many sentences shortened—Theatricals and other amusements—Visit from my brother—Mr. MacLeod

I NEVER had a complaint, except one, against my soldier convicts. While riding one day some distance from the settlement, the superintendent of agriculture, Mr. MacLean, came galloping after me and reported that there was a mutiny amongst the soldier gangs, or rather that they had refused to do their work. I at once rode back to where they were, and found them all idle and standing still. I ordered them to their work, when one of them named Shean (formerly of my own regiment) stepped forward with his hoe in hand (with which farm-implement they were all provided), and in a loud and angry voice attempted to argue their grievance with me. I instantly rode at him, and, with a heavy stick in my hand, knocked him down and rode over him, saying:

"You, who know me long and well, you dare to raise your voice against my authority, you dare to disobey my orders! Get up, and go back at once, every one of you, to your duty!" When he recovered, he begged my pardon, and without another word or murmur they all went back to their work. During this disturbance there were three or four hundred other convicts working in sight, looking on, awaiting the issue, and who doubtless would have joined the soldiers' gangs had anything more serious taken place.

This was the first, the last, and only prisoner I ever had occasion to lift my hand to while on the island. As I have already said, I always found the soldier gangs very willing and obedient, and most thankful for the promise of being trusted with arms should any general outbreak take place which might justify me in calling for their assistance. I had indeed a soldier's feeling for them. For their continued good conduct I recommended many of them at various times to the Government for pardon and restoration to their regiments, which was invariably granted, and among that number was the above-mentioned Daniel Shean, of the 50th Regiment, who afterwards served with me in India, and I found him a good and faithful soldier. He was finally caught and eaten by an alligator in the Ganges, while bathing, on our passage from Chinsurah to Cawnpore in 1842.

It was almost my daily practice to examine and

study the public records and registers of the prisoners and to select from them the names of all men who had for years been noted for good conduct. When I found life prisoners without any charge against them for six or more years, or prisoners of fourteen years behaving well for three or more years, or prisoners of seven years without a fault for two or more years, I recommended them to Government for commutation of their sentence. These recommendations were always attended to and granted, and when received by me were promulgated in my public written orders and read to the prisoners. This had the best effect, and convinced them all that it was never too late to reform, and that the commandant had a constant and friendly eye over all, even the worst of them. When these commuted sentences were without fault, and nearly completed, I had them pardoned altogether and removed to Sydney.

About this time the officers and soldiers of the garrison applied to me to have a temporary theatre erected for them, as they confidently hoped they could make up a respectable "corps dramatique." I entered at once into their wishes, and promised them every encouragement, feeling assured I could not do too much to amuse them; and having plenty of wood and labour at hand, a very comfortable theatre was soon built, with dress boxes and pit, and no sooner finished than our first play was announced. I forget the name of the piece, but our principal performers on that occasion and for many months afterwards were my secretary, the Hon. Mr. Pery, Sergeants Cairns and Duff, Privates Thomas Smith and John Swap, with occasionally Lieutenants Wright, Gregg, and Needham, and some others, and as many minor performers as they needed from the troops. Excellent scenery of all kinds was painted by artists amongst the prisoners, and the orchestra was composed of about half a dozen well-conducted convicts, who played the violin and clarions well. The dresses were generally of coloured calicoes and such other imposing materials as they could find. As the acting was always good, this was a continued source of amusement and delight to us all for years. On one of these nights, in the middle of the performance the "alarm" was sounded. On this occasion many of the performers were acting as women, and of course were dressed accordingly. When an "alarm" is given, no delay is allowed, but all have to assemble as they are. On this night (which by the light of the moon was as clear as day) the "corps dramatique" ran as they were for their arms, and so appeared on the public parade amidst roars of laughter, for their appearance was certainly comic in the extreme, and such a sight of armed warriors in petticoats as never was witnessed before. The "alarm" proved a false one, occasioned by a young soldier firing from his post at the prisoners' barracks on hearing some quarrel amongst the convicts within.

I have already said our roads were excellent all over the island, and the scenery most beautiful and romantic. This encouraged us to pass our time very often in picnics in every direction. There was not a pretty spot at any distance beyond the settlement without a nice bower with tables and seats for our accommodation; and in one or other of these paradises we used to assemble and pass many hours. We had also frequent dinner-parties and dances, and as I had then finished building the new military barracks and hospital, the latter (for we had no sick) made a most excellent and commodious ballroom. The officers of the garrison had a comfortable mess, and were most liberal in their entertainments. In a word, we all agreed well together, and although most of our young men were tired of the limits of our little island, and compared their situation to the monotony and confinement of ship life on a long voyage, I do think we were all very happy, or ought to have been so.

They had also other amusements—fishing, shooting, etc. Phillip Island lay within four miles of us; it is a high land about a mile long, and abounded with wild pigs, wild fowl, and a variety of birds, the most remarkable being the Phillip Island parrots, which were never seen in any other part of Australia. Whenever any of the officers wished for a day's sport there, they had a boat at their command for the day. Starting early, with a good supply of provisions, they were obliged to return before sunset, and generally brought back with them some half-dozen or more pigs, besides other game. In like manner, when they wanted a fishing excursion a boat was provided, and in a few hours they generally returned with dozens of fine fish, caught over known coral rocks. By this time I had an open carriage (made on the island), and as we had many Government horses doing nothing, I wrote to the Colonial Secretary requesting to be allowed to purchase two of them. The answer was that they could not be sold, but that the Governor had no objection to my making use of them as much as I liked. I then sent to Sydney for a double harness, and from that time we had our carriage, and a first-rate (convict) coachman.

In September of this year my dear brother John paid me a visit from India; he was then a colonel of the Madras Army. We had not met for thirty-four years, and our pleasure was now very great in seeing each other. I never saw him again till 1858, and that was our last meeting, for he died soon afterwards at Folkestone.

Reports had now reached Sydney of the better behaviour of our convicts, and we were spoken of with hope and confidence for our continued improvements, so the fear and dread of coming near us, and of residing at Norfolk Island, became daily less. The Rev. Dr. Gregory and Father McEncroe, both of the Roman Catholic Church, offered their services to the Government in Sydney, to go and reside permanently with us, and their services were at once accepted. They came to us by the next trip of the *Governor Phillip*, and right glad was I to receive them. They soon became very popular with us all, and did much good. Then the Government sent down the Rev. Mr. Sharpe, of the Established Church, who on his arrival took charge of our Protestants.

I may here mention that my power was absolute, and that I could remove any of the civil officers at pleasure from the island, but I am happy to say I had but once occasion to exercise my authority. It was officially reported to me that Mr. MacLeod, the superintendent of agriculture, had been trafficking to a considerable extent with the convicts, actually receiving money for them in letters from their friends in Sydney. At first I could not believe this possible. I then got proofs beyond doubt, consisting of letters addressed to Mr. and Mrs. MacLeod from persons in Sydney with several sums of money enclosed for convicts therein named. After some consideration I sent for MacLeod and told him the charges brought against him; he at once boldly denied them, and said there was not the slightest truth in them. I then showed him the letters from Sydney; this staggered and surprised him, but he said he had never seen them before and knew nothing about them. I had no other course left but to suspend him from his duties and send him back to Sydney by the very first opportunity, but it was not till six weeks later that the *Governor Phillip* arrived, and in her he and his family left the island—but before that he gave me some more trouble.

CHAPTER XXII

MANGALORE CATTLE STATION

Wreck of the *Friendship*—I am attacked by Captain Harrison and MacLeod—I receive the Royal Guelphic Order of Knighthood—Secure the sheep and cattle station of "Mangalore" in Port Phillip with my brother—Leave Norfolk Island—Visit to Mangalore

JUST as these charges were brought against MacLeod, the hired schooner *Friendship* arrived off the island with Government provisions and stores, and after exchanging signals she made fast to a large buoy and moorings which had been laid down some months before by his Majesty's ship *Alligator*. Captain Harrison and Mr. Bull then landed to report themselves, and I asked them to dinner. When this was over I told them they must return at once to their ship and look to her safety, that I should send a trusty constable and a few men with them, and that, should it come to blow hard, they must immediately slip away from the moorings and stand out to sea until the weather moderated. They returned to their vessel, but about midnight it blew very hard, and at daylight we had a very strong gale; the schooner was then seen dragging the moorings and drifting fast towards the rocks in front of the settlement, yet not a man could be seen moving on board. I was in bed at this time, and one of my chief constables came and informed me that the schooner was drifting fast on to the rocks, and the surf on the beach was running so high that it was impossible to send out a boat, adding that no man could be seen on board, and that they must all be asleep. I dressed hurriedly, and sent to the military barracks for our gunners and some ammunition for our great guns, and as soon as they arrived we fired round after round over the schooner, yet not a man appeared on deck. At last they heard us, and attempted to make sail. But it was too late; for by this time the ill-fated vessel was amongst the breakers, and in a few minutes more was broadside on the rocks, and soon became a total wreck. The crew and guard got on shore in safety, and our next efforts were to save the cargo, and for this purpose some dozens of prisoners volunteered their services, and went off through the surf, up to their waists, some to their necks, and succeeded in getting on board. Captain Fothergill and about twenty soldiers followed to protect the property and preserve order. There was a large fire seen burning in the caboose on deck, the sparks flying about everywhere, and repeated cries were heard that there was powder on board. The kegs were soon discovered and thrown overboard; the prisoners then got into the hold, and managed to get small and large cases of stores on deck, then handed them over the ship's side to gangs of prisoners on the rocks. In this manner the whole cargo was safely landed without any loss or damage, but the unfortunate ship became a greater wreck every day. At last what remained of her was towed into the boat harbour, and several attempts were made to patch her up, but all to no purpose, and at last all efforts were abandoned.

I had to quarter Captain Harrison, his crew and passengers on the different civil and military officers and free constables, and I took Mr. and Mrs. Bull to Government House. Captain Harrison became the guest of the military officers, and we all endeavoured to make them as comfortable as we possibly could. About a month afterwards it was reported to me that Captain Harrison talked of selling the wreck and other materials and stores belonging to the vessel, and that MacLeod, the late superintendent, was in his confidence, and was advising him to do so. I took no notice of this at the time, but from other information I clearly saw the object was to defraud the underwriters, as the ship was insured. Captain Harrison had posted handbills over the settlement, naming a day for the sale of the wreck and stores by public auction. I ordered the bills to be torn down, and, sending for Captain Harrison, I reprimanded him for attempting such proceedings without my order, and told him I could not permit any sale of the kind, but that when an opportunity offered for sending him and his crew back to Sydney they should be allowed free passages and room for his stores and cargo also. He appeared dissatisfied, and wished to argue the matter with me, saying that he and others thought it better to sell everything on the island. I begged to know his advisers, but he would not tell me, and from this time he gave me much trouble.

At last the *Governor Phillip* was reported in sight. I ordered Captain Harrison and his crew and passengers to embark in her for Sydney, and so got rid of them after a detention of seventy days. I also sent MacLeod away beyond my control for ever, and our mail contained my reports to the Government of the wreck, and all details connected with the saving of the cargo, the attempt to sell the wreck and stores by public auction, and my refusal to allow Captain Harrison to do this. I also reported the whole of MacLeod's misconduct, and that I had suspended him from his situation and sent him back to Sydney. I had the satisfaction to receive the Governor's entire approval of all these proceedings. Soon after this several letters appeared in the Sydney papers abusing me, reflecting on my "misgovernment" of Norfolk Island, and complaining of my treatment of the captain, crew, and passengers of the schooner *Friendship*. I was afterwards assured these letters were written, some by Captain Harrison, others by MacLeod and Mr. Bull, who with his wife left me and Mrs. Anderson with many tears and endless professions of gratitude for our kindness and hospitality during their long stay with us. Of these letters I took not the slightest notice.

Early in 1838 I received a public notification that his Majesty King William IV was graciously pleased to appoint me a Knight of the Royal Hanoverian Guelphic Order for my past services in the field; at the same time I received the Golden Star and Ribbon of the Order. I was indeed proud of this distinction, as it was conferred without any application from me, and I was included in a list of many brave officers specially selected by his Majesty from different regiments for this mark of his royal favour.

Soon after this I received a letter from my brother John, recommending that we should together take up a station for sheep and cattle in the newly discovered district of Port Phillip, saying that he was willing to purchase a few hundred sheep and cattle to make a beginning, if I could find trustworthy persons to go and take up a suitable run and the charge and management of the establishment afterwards, and that he wished to include amongst the number to be employed a Mr. Howell, a young *protégé* of his. My brother-in-law, Septimus Campbell, had some time before this expressed a wish to retire from the service and try what he could do as a squatter, so I named this chance to him, and offered to recommend him to my brother for the management, and for a share in the concern hereafter if he proved himself capable and deserving of the charge. He willingly accepted, and I wrote accordingly to my brother; I named also three men then in Sydney, who had been until lately prisoners at Norfolk Island. I knew they were not only trustworthy, but also well acquainted with sheep and cattle, as they had been formerly employed as shepherds on sheep and cattle stations. My brother wrote back approval of my proposal and consenting to give Campbell the management of our station, provided he could at once enter on the charge, as he was already in treaty for the purchase of a few hundred sheep. Campbell now sent in his application to retire from the service by the sale of his commission, and I gave him leave to return by the *Governor Phillip* (then with us) to Sydney, and there he found my brother and Mr. Howell. At that time convict servants were assigned by the Government to officers in numbers according to their rank, and Campbell made an application in my name, and in his own, for three men whom I had named, Joseph Underwood, William Percival, and Richard Glegg. They were at once granted, and most thankful they were for our confidence.

My brother now concluded his bargain for the purchase of a few hundred sheep, a dray and team of working bullocks, and a variety of stores and farm implements, etc.; and having made his arrangements with Campbell, and given him a few hundred pounds for the purchase of cattle, they started for Port Phillip about October, 1838. They went overland, except Campbell, who had decided on going by sea, so as to get down before them. For the first week the overland party got on very well, but after that they had endless difficulties and losses, for Howell gave himself up entirely to drink and was seldom sober, and when his money was expended he actually sold some of the bullocks and sheep. He frequently remained for days and nights at miserable pot-houses quite insensible from intoxication, and when he became sober he was not allowed to leave till he had paid for his folly by giving up as many of his sheep and bullocks as the equally drunken and unprincipled landlord chose to extort from him. Fortunately, our men remained steady, especially Underwood, who now took the lead and the entire charge of our property, and with the other men watched the animals day and night, and never left them; but in spite of all this they lost a number of sheep. Some were stolen, some were knocked up and died, from bad roads and much rain.

At last, after a long journey of two months, Underwood and his two men reached the bank of the Goulburn River, in the Port Phillip district, with about three hundred and fifty of our sheep, the dray, and three or four of our bullocks. They had not seen Howell for some weeks before, and he was drunk at a public-house when they last saw him. Underwood determined on halting and taking possession until the arrival of Campbell. Meantime Howell joined them, but left them again in a few days for a public-house which was on the Sydney line of road, a few miles distant. Campbell directed them to stay where they were, on our future run and station, and to try and extend the boundaries as far as they could, taking care to mark the limits as well as possible, and to report to him by marks or other signs the extent of country they wished to take up, so as to enable him to make a special application to the Government for our right and title to the same. Underwood managed this admirably, and, having had a good knowledge of sheep stations before, he took care to give us a wide range. In front we had seventeen miles on the banks of the Goulburn River, and from twenty to thirty miles in all directions back. By a survey made a few years afterwards, our run was computed at about eighty-five thousand acres. I named the place at once Mangalore, in compliment to my brother, that being the name of his military station in India, of which he was very fond, and so it remains on all charts to this day.

Campbell never stayed at Mangalore, as some pressing business obliged him to go to Van Diemen's Land, and thence to Sydney; so for many months our station and property remained under the nominal care of Howell, but in reality under the faithful management of Joseph Underwood. There was little now to do, for when we took possession there was not one other settler in that neighbourhood, nor nearer than the Devil's River, a distance of more than a hundred miles. There was a miserable public-house and a small store in our neighbourhood known as Seymour, and there all sorts of supplies and provisions could be purchased at exorbitant prices, and they were always ready to trust squatters or their agents, so that Howell had no difficulty in getting what he required. I was still at Norfolk Island during this time, and knew nothing of Howell's doings for many months later. My brother had returned to India, confident with me that all would be well at Mangalore, and telling me, as his last instruction, that I was to consider the whole as a joint speculation, and keep an account of all additional expenditure. I wrote to

MANGALORE CATTLE STATION 183

Campbell and authorized him to draw upon me for any money he required.

We remained happily at Norfolk Island until February, 1839. About the end of the month the *Governor Phillip* arrived, bringing a detachment of the 80th Regiment under the command of Major Bunbury to relieve the 50th, and with dispatches to me naming the major as my successor as civil superintendent and military commandant of the island.

After our arrival at Sydney I began to hear something about our sheep station and the doings at Mangalore, and that Howell was constantly drunk; so I made up my mind to go to Port Phillip and Mangalore. I left Sydney in a sailing vessel in December, 1839, for Melbourne, and arrived there after a week's journey. Melbourne was then little more than a village, and with only two or three very humble so-called hotels. On my landing I was so fortunate as to meet a Mr. Michael Scobie, from my own birthplace, whom I had known as a boy; he told me that my worthless superintendent Howell was then, and for some time had been, in Melbourne, and constantly drunk. Mr. Scobie accompanied me to search for him, and we soon discovered that he lived in a miserable pot-house called the Lamb Inn. He must have heard of my arrival and seen us approaching, for as we entered he escaped through the back door. After many more hunts we at last got hold of him, and I insisted on his going with us on our journey the next morning. In two days we arrived at Mangalore, where we found our true and trusty men, Underwood, Percival and Glegg, evidently doing their best, but suffering a little from want of tea and sugar and a scarcity of flour. Next day they collected the sheep, and Scobie made a minute muster of all. They were reported all healthy and in good order. He next rode with me round every part of the station, and the more he saw the more he was pleased with the character and capabilities of the run. What we heard from the men and saw for ourselves convinced us that Howell was not to be trusted in any way with the management of such an undertaking, and that the sooner I got rid of him the better. I now appealed to Scobie, and offered him his own terms if he would remain at Mangalore and take charge. He first said he would willingly oblige me, but that he had a small station of his own near Melbourne, and that therefore he must take time to consider my proposal. We remained a week longer at Mangalore; Scobie occupied himself during the whole of that time in riding about and gaining additional information. He then consented to remain with me for one year certain, for £100, and one-third of my increase of lambs, provided that I would allow him to return to Melbourne with me for a few days to settle his own affairs. I consented, and we at once signed a written agreement, and Howell was told his services as manager were dispensed with, but that he could remain at the station on a small salary as long as he conducted himself properly and made himself useful, but if not, Scobie had my authority to dismiss him at once. We then returned to Melbourne very much pleased with our arrangements.

CHAPTER XXIII

ON MY DEFENCE

Court of inquiry as to my management of Norfolk Island—Major Bunbury reprimanded by Commander-in-Chief at the Horse Guards for his unfounded charges

I SHOULD have mentioned sooner that when I left Sydney a dispatch was received by the major-general commanding from Major Bunbury, reporting a serious outbreak and mutiny amongst his detachment at Norfolk Island, and that Sir Maurice O'Connell had determined to relieve the 80th at once from Norfolk Island by an equal number again of the 50th Regiment. I was sent for by the governor, and also by the general; and although they gave me no particulars of Major Bunbury's dispatch, I was asked many questions about the soldiers' gardens, when and why they were given to the men, and my opinion respecting them. All this I explained, and said they were established by me with the authority and approval of the late governor, Sir Richard Bourke, as a means not only of amusement and employment for the soldiers on the settlement, but also in order to give them a constant supply of good vegetables. I was then told by the general that he was determined to relieve Major Bunbury and to send Major Ryan in command. I was not allowed to know more, but I heard it whispered that the outbreak was in consequence of Major Bunbury depriving the soldiers of their gardens and ordering them to be charged a trifle daily for vegetables from the Government gardens, and that, the soldiers having resisted, he actually sent gangs of convicts to root up and destroy the gardens, which at once made the soldiers fly to their arms and drive the convicts away, in open defiance of Major Bunbury's presence and authority. It was also hinted that he blamed me for all this in having granted these gardens to the soldiers, which he considered contrary to, and subversive of, good order and discipline.

Having heard these whispers, I called upon the general and requested I might be informed whether Major Bunbury had attempted to blame me for the open defiance of his authority by his own men. The general again said he could not then enter into any further explanation, but that I should hear all when Major Bunbury returned; I was therefore obliged to be satisfied so far, and I took my leave. Meantime a ship was chartered and ready to take Major Ryan and his detachment to Norfolk Island, and she was to be escorted by

H.M.S. *Rattlesnake*, to force a landing if necessary. In a few days I left Sydney, and did not go back for ten days after Major Bunbury had returned, and the first news I heard was that he had not confined nor punished even one man for the mutiny, which displeased the general very much. Fifteen soldiers were then arrested as the ringleaders and placed in confinement, and in due course were brought to trial charged with mutiny. They were all found guilty and sentenced to transportation for life. I was also informed that Major Bunbury, in his evidence, did not hesitate to blame me for all these irregularities, and for the insubordination and mutiny of his own men! which he stated were the result of "the relaxed order and system and total absence of military discipline" which I had allowed on the island. This was the substance of his evidence, and as I was absent from Sydney during the sitting of the court-martial, my friends took care to tell me of it on my return.

I went at once to Sir Maurice O'Connell and complained, and I requested an immediate court of inquiry into my system and the efficiency or otherwise of my command. The general hesitated, and said he saw no necessity for any such inquiry, as he was perfectly satisfied; but I said I was not, and that as every one had heard Major Bunbury's serious charges against me, it was no more than justice to me, and to my reputation and character

ON MY DEFENCE

as an officer, that an immediate inquiry should take place. He then consented to order a court of inquiry, and next day Lieut.-Colonel French, Major Cotton, and a major whose name I forget, were named for this duty, and directed to "inquire into the system and discipline maintained by Major Anderson during his command at Norfolk Island."

I was allowed to make a statement in detail of my system, daily duties, and discipline. I then called in succession Captains Petit, Fothergill, and Lieutenants Sheaffe and Needham, who served for years with me on the island, and each of these officers stated to the court "that no commanding officer could have been more zealous and attentive to his own duties and to the efficiency of his detachment; that his parades were regular every morning and evening; that the conduct of the detachment was so uniformly good and regular that not more than two or three soldiers were brought to trial while the 50th was at Norfolk Island; that the detachment was inspected once a month, and the barracks and messes were regularly visited by Major Anderson; that if possible he was too strict rather than too easy with his officers and men." Major Bunbury was allowed to cross-examine each of these officers, but could get nothing from them in support of his unfounded charges. The next officer called was Colonel Woodhouse, commanding the 50th Regiment, who informed the court that he "always considered Major

Anderson an able and efficient officer, that he received constant reports of the good conduct and discipline of his detachment, and that whenever he had any troublesome officers or soldiers he always sent them to Norfolk Island to be schooled by Major Anderson." The next called was Lieutenant and Adjutant Tudor, who spoke to the same effect. Last of all I called Major Hunter, the major of brigade in Sydney, and he stated that nothing could have been more satisfactory than the official reports from Norfolk Island, and that he had heard from many that the detachment was considered to be in the highest possible state of good order and discipline. I here declined calling any more evidence.

Major Bunbury was then requested to state whether he wished to say anything more, or to call any evidence. He first recalled Captains Petit and Fothergill, and asked them whether they did not think the giving of gardens to the soldiers injurious to military discipline and to their drill and proper appearance as soldiers; they said, "Certainly not." He next asked them whether the soldiers did not sell their gardens to their successors. They answered that they sold their crops, which they themselves had grown and laboured for, but not their gardens. He then called in one or two of his own sergeants, but the only thing he could get out of them was that the soldiers of the 80th Regiment had paid the soldiers

ON MY DEFENCE

of the 50th for the gardens, and therefore considered them their private property. Major Bunbury declined to call in any of his own officers. After some further debate the proceedings were closed. Here we were all ordered to withdraw, and the court was closed for the recording of its final opinion.

I was not then allowed to know what that was, but from the clear and most satisfactory evidence which had been given on my behalf there could only be one opinion on the subject, and it was certainly a most gratifying victory. A few days more confirmed this view of the case. I therefore went to the general and said that I had waited patiently, expecting he would publicly promulgate the opinion of the court of inquiry, but to my surprise he said he saw no necessity for doing so. I told him this did not at all satisfy me, that I felt I had a right to request he would promulgate the opinion of the court, but all my endeavours to this effect failed. I then asked him if I was at liberty to proclaim the substance of my present interview with him. He said, "Most certainly," and on the same day I took care to do so. From that day I had no further intercourse with Major Bunbury.

Many months afterwards, while in India, I received an official notification from the major of brigade in Sydney that the Commander-in-Chief at the Horse Guards had approved of the proceedings of the court of inquiry, and had directed the major-general commanding in Sydney to convey a severe reprimand to Major Bunbury, and to inform him that " if he attempted again to insinuate any such charges against Major Anderson he would be brought before a general court-martial."

CHAPTER XXIV

ORDERED TO CALCUTTA

50th Regiment ordered to India—Sudden death of one of my boys—Voyage to India—First experiences of Calcutta

I CONTINUED to receive good accounts of our station from Scobie, and nothing remarkable occurred during the remainder of that year, until I visited Mangalore to see for myself what he was doing. Having procured six weeks' leave, I left Sydney with Major Serjeantson, and in a few days reached Melbourne. We hired horses, and found our way in two days to Mangalore. I then made a partial inspection of many of our flocks and herds of cattle, and of the improvements that Scobie had made, and was very much pleased with all I saw and heard, and especially with the large increase of lambs and calves. Everything was most satisfactory. I saw at once that I could not have a better manager, and therefore, with the fullest confidence in him, renewed the contract for another year.

On my return to Sydney the first news I heard

was that my regiment was about to embark for India. I landed and hurried at once to the barracks, and discovered this to be true, and all preparations already in progress for our embarkation. I found my dear wife and children quite well, but all very sad and excited, and wondering if I should be back in time. This was about the middle of January, 1841, and I arranged with my wife that she and the children should remain in New South Wales until I could leave the service and return to them. We also settled that the two boys should remain at Sydney College, and that my wife, with the other children, should remove and live at Windsor (thirty miles from Sydney). My two boys accompanied me to the ship, and ran back in all haste to be in time at the College for their lessons, and no doubt got uncomfortably heated; but they returned to their lodgings without complaining. About two o'clock next morning we were roused by the landlord, who came to tell us they were both very ill, and that we had better send a doctor immediately. I at once went to our assistant-surgeon, Dr. Ellison, and requested him to go as quickly as possible to see them; he did so, and told us they had scarlatina, which was then very common in Sydney. They became worse, and with the advice of the doctor we brought them home, and now their dear mother gave her whole thought and attention to them; but there was a continued change for the worse, and both became insensible.

The 80th Regiment from Parramatta marched into our Sydney barracks. They asked me and my officers to dine with them, and I went, with a very heavy heart, as I was in great anxiety about my boys. Just as the cloth was removed one of the waiters told me my servant wanted me, and on going to him he said, without any preparation or hesitation, "Master Johnny is dead, sir." I ran home at once, and the sobs of my dear wife confirmed the sad tale. I went with her into the room, and there they both lay, the one dead, the other unconscious, yet I could scarcely believe the fact, for our beloved Johnny was still warm. No medical man was present when he died, nor was his mother or nurse aware that his soul had fled, till they observed he had ceased to breathe. Our agony and sorrow may be imagined but not described. We retired to bed but not to sleep, and had not been long there before the nurse came and said that she did not believe the child was dead, as he was still warm. I instantly flew to the room, but, alas! her hopes were only a delusion. Next morning we determined on removing the other children, and our good friend W. H. Wright took them at once to his residence at Clarendon House, near Windsor, where my wife was to follow them with our dear boy Acland, should God in His mercy be pleased to spare him.

After this sad and most unexpected bereavement, our quarters became indeed a house of desolation, and the more so from the fact that I was to leave my wife alone and helpless in her sorrow and continued fears for our only son.

Our ships were now ready to sail, but were detained by contrary winds. This delay gave me a little respite, and enabled me to go to Sir Maurice O'Connell to submit to his consideration my helpless situation and my grief, and above all the lonely position of my poor wife, and my hope that he would grant me leave of absence pending my expected promotion, and so allow the regiment to go on to Calcutta, where it would be under the command of Major Ryan, who was to arrive from England at that time. The general heard me with evident sympathy, and expressed his sincere regret for me and for my wife, but would not grant my request. He said that on delivering over my regiment in Calcutta I might then get leave of absence and return, on sending in my application to retire from the service by the sale of my commission. Our boy Acland continued in the same uncertain state between life and death, and was still insensible when I left.

Days and days did I brood over my fears and misery, and I could not conceal my grief. My brother-officers and the ladies on board tried to rouse and amuse me. They were gay without a care, and every evening amused themselves dancing on the quarter-deck. Our voyage was unusually long and tedious. The only cause of excitement which I can remember was that while off Cape Lewin we caught an albatross one fine morning, with a 50th button tied round his neck by a piece of string; this convinced us our other ship, the *Lady MacNaughton*, must be ahead of us, and that our unfortunate captive must have been handled by some of our people before, for in no other way could a 50th button get attached to the neck of an albatross on the wide ocean. Of course we let our prisoner go free again.

On the 17th May we arrived and anchored in the Hooghly. Early next morning we disembarked and marched into Fort William, and were welcomed by Major Ryan and other friends. After this we endeavoured to make ourselves as comfortable as we could in our respective quarters. Mine were with Major Ryan, in a suite of very good and commodious rooms, but the heat was so intolerable that we had neither comfort nor rest. We suffered from the heat fearfully, though wearing only the lightest possible clothing, and from utter exhaustion we expected almost every moment to breathe our last. Next morning we had a visit from the fort major, Major Douglass, who had been for many years in India, and he at once asked us why our punkahs were not going. We said we did not know how to work them. Then, observing our punkah wallas sitting idle in a corner, he "pitched into" them, and abused them for not doing their work; they at once answered they only waited for our orders, and then commenced to pull. In a moment our rooms were full of refreshing and pure air. We then could breathe freely, and from that hour became more reconciled to our lot.

Major Douglass then asked me if I had visited Lord Auckland, the Governor-General, and Sir Jasper Nicoll, the Commander-in-Chief. He recommended me to go at once and report myself and pay my respects to them. He then ordered a palkee and told the bearers to take me to Government House, and then to the residence of Sir Jasper Nicoll, and back to the Fort. I had to dress in full uniform; the heat was fearful; my thick padded coat was most distressing to me, and I got alarmed, having more than once heard of people being found dead in their palkees from the heat. My bearers, quite unconscious of my fears, jogged on and carried me in safety to the Commander-in-Chief's residence. I was received by Sir Jasper and Lady Nicoll, and after half an hour's conversation about my regiment and voyage I took my leave. At Government House I was most kindly received by Lord Auckland and his sisters, and our conversation was much on the same subject, and I then returned to my quarters.

My first dinner at Government House appeared to me very imposing. The grand apartments were truly splendid. There was a magnificent display of plate—the countless native attendants were most brilliantly arrayed, and all the Oriental splendour round us was dazzling in the extreme. Yet with all this I sat without any dinner for some time, though every one else was being waited on by one or two of their own kitmutgars. Not one of these numerous servants offered to wait on me! At last the young lady who sat at my right asked me if I had no kitmutgar present. I told her I had not, as I was not aware that I could bring my servant to Government House. She then begged me to allow hers to wait on me, and told me that the custom was to take our kitmutgars to attend upon us, at all dinners or other parties.

CHAPTER XXV

LIFE AT CALCUTTA

Magnificent entertainments at Calcutta—Dost Mahomet—Wreck of the *Ferguson*—Preparations for Burmese campaign—Special favour shown to soldiers of the 50th Regiment

AT Government House the balls were really magnificent, and well worth seeing. The company, of English ladies and gentlemen and of military men in resplendent uniforms, was numerous, but scores of native princes and rajahs, and wealthy baboos in the most splendid dresses and covered with jewels, also constantly attended these brilliant assemblies and gave a wonderfully dazzling effect. The suite of dancing-halls was magnificent, with marble floors, and with dozens of punkahs constantly going to keep all cool and comfortable; and there the young and the gay danced at their ease and without the usual European exertion, from eleven until an early hour in the morning.

The most conspicuous and splendid person at

all these parties was Dost Mahomet, the ex-ruler of Afghanistan, who was then a State prisoner at Calcutta. He and his numerous suite were paid the most marked and courtly attentions by the Governor-General, and always invited to every ball or dinner-party, and there, and everywhere else, he was received and treated with all the honours due to a sovereign, and he gained by his courtly manners and easy bearing the respect and goodwill of every Englishman who came near him. He always appeared amongst the crowd in his carriage, every morning and evening in the public course at Fort William, and was invariably saluted by every officer and Englishman, and all these greetings he returned with visible satisfaction. Many if not all the British officers would have gone further and called upon him to show their respect (for he was much liked by every one), but this was forbidden by a Government order, and none but natives were permitted to visit him; these visitors, however, were constant, many princes and rajahs from all parts of India coming daily.

About this time I was invited by the Governor-General to spend a few days with him at his country residence at Barrackpore, and on the first day of my visit the newspapers announced the arrival of a ship from Sydney. This was great news for me, for I made sure of a letter from my dear wife, and having said so to Lord

Auckland, I begged to be allowed to take my leave. He most kindly pressed me to remain, and said he would dispatch a man at once for my letters; but I was too impatient, so after thanking them for their kindness I started in all haste for Calcutta, but on my arrival found no letter for me. This was indeed a sad disappointment, and my restless mind at once attributed this silence to the worst and most melancholy cause. After a trying suspense of six months, I received a letter from Major Serjeantson enclosing a long and cheering one from my wife, assuring me of our dear boy Acland's recovery and perfect health, and that she and all the children were quite well and had removed to Windsor, where she had taken a comfortable house. I was again happy and most thankful, and my great desire was to write to my wife to assure her of my joy, and my gratitude to God. But there was then no prospect of any direct ship for Australia, so I was obliged to write viâ London.

My present letter, sent through Major Serjeantson, was written in April, three months after I had parted with my family, and it will be remembered that when we left Sydney that officer remained there with his own company and our sick then in hospital, and in expectation of receiving and bringing on to Calcutta a number of recruits for the regiment shortly expected from

England. With these detachments and some young officers, Major Serjeantson embarked at Sydney on board the ship *Ferguson* at the end of April; but while coming through Torres Straits they were wrecked, and must have all perished, but for the fortunate chance of two other ships being in company with them. These followed the *Ferguson*, which took the lead through a narrow channel, and had just time to bring up and anchor when she struck, and immediately fired guns of distress. This happened before daylight, at four o'clock in the morning. The boats from the other ships were immediately sent to assist, but the sea began at once to break over the *Ferguson*, and for some time so violently that the boats could not and dared not approach her, and for a time they were obliged to keep at a distance, looking on only. At last, during a lull, they managed to get a rope conveyed from the *Ferguson* to the boats, and by that means another and another. Her long boat was then got into slings and hoisted over the side high up above water. Mrs. Serjeantson and all the women and children were put into it, and after a given signal it was lowered into the sea, the ropes from the other boats having been made fast to it, and then it was hurriedly hauled and dragged through the surf until it reached them in safety. After many cheers they were taken to the other ships and made, so far as possible, comfortable, but after that the sea became so rough that nothing more could be done that day, and in continued fear and suspense both parties remained watching each other until dark.

For the rest of that long sad night the agony and fears of both the rescued and of those more numerous ones still on the wreck may be imagined. It must have been a truly dreadful position. Happily, next morning the sea was more settled, but still too rough and dangerous for boats to go alongside, though by pluck and daring energy they managed to get in succession under the bowsprit of the *Ferguson*, from which man after man of the soldiers and crew were dropped into the boats without any greater accident than a heavy sea breaking occasionally over some of them. This was done from the duty muster rolls, every man in his regular turn and without any confusion, and my dear friend Major Serjeantson, and the captain, Verity, were the last who left the ill-fated *Ferguson*—all reaching the other two ships in safety. But they unfortunately lost nearly the whole of their baggage.

We had now been a few months in India, and some of our officers and many of our men were sick in barracks and in hospital, and a considerable number were suddenly carried off. Major Turner was the first officer who died, and was soon followed by Ensigns Kelly and Heaton. This was during the rainy season; when that passed away the regiment became more healthy.

In October of the same year I was sent for by the Governor-General and told there was every prospect of war with Burma, and that he feared an attack on our position and garrison at Moulmein, in the Tenasserim province, so he had determined to reinforce that station at once. He then asked how soon I could get my regiment ready for embarkation. I answered, "In an hour, without difficulty or inconvenience." He smiled and appeared much pleased, but said he thought that was impossible. I replied that we were always ready, and could embark the same evening if necessary. He then ordered me to go at once to the Marine Board, to put myself in communication with them, and to let them know I was ready to embark my regiment at the shortest notice, whenever the transports were prepared to receive us. I did so, and was told I might make my preparations and expect further orders in the course of that day or the next. A few hours afterwards the orders were issued for the following morning, and punctual to the hour we were at the wharf at daylight, and there found boats to take us to our ships. Mine was a large Government steamer, in which our headquarters and eight companies were embarked, and the remaining two companies were received on board a sailing ship, under command of Major Serjeantson, who had succeeded to a majority on the death of Major Turner. Lord Auckland and his staff attended at the wharf to see us off. My fine regiment was in the most splendid order—not a man was absent, and all as steady as rocks—and reached our ships without the slightest confusion or accident. I was afterwards told that the Governor-General and his staff expressed their admiration of the steady and soldier-like appearance of the regiment, and their wonder and surprise at not seeing one drunken man amongst them; this was so unusual at former embarkations that Lord Auckland actually asked whether Colonel Anderson did not screen his drunken men by keeping them confined in the Fort!

I shall not name the regiment which we relieved on our first arrival at Fort William, but I saw them embarking at the same place, and I well remember my amazement at seeing dozens of the men not only drunk but most riotous and mutinous in conduct and language to their officers. This reminds me of another most creditable contrast between the conduct of the gallant 50th and what I was assured by the best authority had been the conduct of another regiment and other corps previously quartered in Fort William. On our arrival there I found the standing-orders required that every soldier should return to the Fort by sunset, and that none should be permitted, without written passes, to be absent after that time. I considered this a most unnecessary check to the recreations and reasonable enjoyment of good and well-behaved soldiers, and represented this to the consideration of the principal staff officer of the Fort, Colonel Warren; but all my arguments had no effect on that stern and prejudiced officer, who had held his appointment for many years, and strongly maintained that such were the standing-orders of the Fort, and that they could not be changed.

Seeing I had no chance with Colonel Warren, I went direct to Lord Auckland and stated my opinion to him. He heard me with attention, but I soon saw he also was opposed to my wishes, and unwilling to deviate from an old-established standing-order. I told him I thought it was a great restraint upon good soldiers, and that I had heard the men of former regiments in the Fort were in the habit of lowering themselves by ropes and blankets from the walls into the moat, and so escaping; that, in my opinion, such confinement was enough to make bad men worse, and that if his lordship would only make the trial and trust me and my men, by allowing me to give a certain number of written passes for a few hours each night, I would pledge myself to be responsible for their good conduct in town, and for their punctual return to the Fort at the hour required. He hesitated for some time, and, though surprised at my great confidence in my men, he at last gave in, and next day a general order was issued "granting this indulgence on trial, at the special request of

Colonel Anderson." That very evening I granted passes till eleven o'clock, and continued to do so daily while we remained at Fort William, without ever having cause to regret it. More than once Lord Auckland expressed his perfect satisfaction and his approbation of the measure; but I never heard if this indulgence was continued to other corps after we left.

CHAPTER XXVI

AT MOULMEIN

Great welcome to Moulmein—No fighting after all—The Madras native regiments

WE now sailed for Moulmein, and found there the 63rd Regiment and four strong and splendid regiments of Madras Native Infantry—all under the command of Brigadier-General Logan, late of the Rifle Brigade, and now of the 63rd Regiment. There was also a considerable force of European and Madras artillery, engineers, and commissariat, and a very imposing naval force under Admiral Cooper.

Our residence at Moulmein was very comfortable and agreeable to us all; the climate was cool and bracing, and under the hospitable rule of our most able and kind brigadier we soon became all intimate and friendly, and the most social dinner-parties at our messes and at the brigadier's became the order of the day. All the Madras regiments had excellent mess establishments, equal in every respect to the Queen's, and their constant and liberal hospitality could not be surpassed by any of our corps. A few days after our arrival in garrison the four Madras regiments invited me and the officers of the 50th Regiment to dinner, and for this purpose they pitched and joined their four mess marquees together into one splendid pavilion, the interior decorated with garlands and evergreens tastefully arranged, and with the spaces filled up with arms and military trophies. The tables were covered with the most brilliant plate and glass, and the lights were numerous and magnificent. All round the outside was a double row of natives, double torchbearers, filling up the intervals between the sentries and the bands of the regiments stationed on each side of this stupendous marquee. The effect was truly brilliant and imposing, and no one could approach the gathering without wonder and delight.

We sat down, in all, nearly a hundred officers. The dinner and the wines were excellent, and the attendance of so unusual a number of active native servants in their thin white muslin robes and coloured turbans and kummerbunds was really imposing, and something new to us at a military mess. When dinner was over, and after the usual loyal toasts, the president stood up and proposed a bumper to the health and welcome of Colonel Anderson and the officers of the 50th Regiment. This was drunk with much applause and deafening

cheers, the band playing "John Anderson, my joe."
I then rose and thanked them with much sincerity
from myself and my officers for their hearty welcome and good wishes, and as they all knew my
dear brother, Lieut.-General John Anderson, of
their own army, I said I felt the more gratified
and flattered from the conviction that their
good feelings towards me individually were more
from their regard for my brother than from any
good they could discover in me, and that I was
equally free to confess he was indeed much the
better man of the two; and here I was interrupted by one of them standing up and shouting
aloud, "A d—d deal better fellow than ever you
will be!" I instantly turned towards the speaker
and told him, and all, that a more gratifying compliment could not be paid me, and that I should not
fail to assure my brother of the very flattering and
friendly feeling which was thus so publicly expressed
towards him. Three cheers then followed for " Old
Jock Anderson!" and, not yet satisfied, they now
(half a dozen of them) got me out of my chair and on
their shoulders, and so carried me round and round
the table amidst deafening cheers. The evening
continued one of the most social and merriest of
my life, and dinner after dinner followed at each of
our messes, and many quiet ones also were enjoyed
in succession at the married officers' quarters, and
always on a large scale at the brigadier's once
a fortnight, where that good man and Mrs. Logan

made every one happy and at home by their kind and courteous manner and genuine hospitality.

Our military duties were not less exciting and, to me, not less pleasing. We had grand field days and sham fights once a fortnight, with all the troops in garrison present, and I never saw any man handle his force more ably or more effectually than Brigadier Logan. It was quite a treat and a lesson to be manœuvred by that able and gallant officer. He was a soldier every inch of him, and his ardent zeal for the service was part of his character, but his then most anxious wishes and the object of our expedition to Moulmein were defeated, for although we were ever ready and expecting an attack every morning from the Burmese, they never dared to come near us. The river Salwen or Martaban (from two to three miles broad) separated the contending forces, for it will be seen by reference to a map that Moulmein is situated on the left bank of the Salwen River, about twenty miles from the sea, and the town and fortress of Martaban, which was then strongly occupied by the enemy, immediately opposite on the right bank of the river, and it was from that place that we expected an attack every morning in boats. We could see their troops distinctly every day parading and marching about in large bodies, with their drums playing and their colours flying, and always with a large fleet of boats moored under their fortifications, as if prepared and meditating a descent. And they could also see our men-of-war and their armed boats pulling about and doing night guard ready to receive them.

In this way we continued for months staring at each other, but in the meantime we made ourselves more comfortable by covering all our tents with matting, which protected us not only from the rains and heavy dews which are common there, but also from the heat and glare of the sun during the day, and we occasionally enjoyed ourselves by exploring and picnic parties in the men-of-war's armed boats up the river; for we were always on the most happy and intimate terms with the officers of our little navy, dining with them now and then and having them as our guests repeatedly. In a word, our sojourn at Moulmein was a very happy and jolly one. We never knew positively the cause of the enemy's hesitation in making an attempt to attack us, but we heard that one or two flags of truce had been sent from our Government at Calcutta up the Irrawaddy with dispatches to Ava for the Burmese Government, and we concluded that terms of amity and peace had been proposed and perhaps agreed to, and this became the more probable when, early in March, 1842, orders were received for the immediate return of the 50th Regiment to Calcutta.

We were indeed sorry to leave Moulmein—the climate was so much cooler and better than India; and we had made so many kind and agreeable friends that to part with them—perhaps for ever —was far from pleasant. A more than usual intimacy took place between our men and the soldiers of the Madras Native Infantry, and they were frequently seen walking and chatting together. Most of these fine-looking men knew and served repeatedly under their own "General Anderson" —and they soon saw by our strong family likeness that I was his brother, and whenever any of them passed me they not only saluted but gave me a warm recognizing smile. When I first saw them I was struck by their fine manly and soldier-like appearance, superior in every way to the Bengal native troops and evidently under better discipline, and now the best proof of this is that when the whole of the Bengal native troops, cavalry, artillery, and infantry, mutinied, and murdered their English officers in cold blood, not one single corps of the Madras native army wavered for a minute. They remained faithful and true to their salt and to their colours, although it was well known, and beyond all doubt, that the leaders of the Bengal mutiny had sent many emissaries and appeals for aid to them.

CHAPTER XXVII

VOYAGE UP THE GANGES

Return to Calcutta—Much illness in regiment—Boat journey of three months to Cawnpore—Incidents of the voyage—Death of Daniel Shean

I CANNOT at this moment recollect how we left Moulmein, and here, for the first time since I commenced this narrative, my memory fails me, but I think it was in sailing ships, for I remember that on our arrival off Fort William we were transhipped into country boats next day, and proceeded with the tide up the Hooghly and landed at Chinsurah. There we found Colonel Woodhouse, from Sydney, and a large detachment of recruits and young officers from England under Captain Fothergill, and, what was far more acceptable to me, letters from my dear wife with cheering accounts of herself and my dear children.

I now as a matter of course gave over the command of the regiment to Colonel Woodhouse, and for a time I was, comparatively speaking, an idle man. He, being a full colonel and of so many years' standing, was entitled by the orders of the army in India to the local rank of major-general, and to a separate command. Therefore I felt sure of getting the regiment again before long. We now got into the month of April, and the heat was great and most cruelly trying. We spoke much of the delightful climate of Moulmein, and of the dear friends whom we had left behind us there. The heat and the change of climate soon produced much sickness amongst our officers and men. Fever and cholera prevailed, and we lost many men and Assistant-Surgeon McBean from the latter fearful malady. He was quite well and dined at the mess the night of his death. He sat opposite to me and was in high spirits, and I observed he ate heartily and stayed at table for an hour or two afterwards. On retiring to his room he was suddenly seized with cholera at about two o'clock in the morning, and died in agony soon afterwards. He was buried the same day.

In June we had a fearful storm, or rather a hurricane, lasting two days and nights. Much damage was done, and many ships and river craft driven on shore and totally lost, but it cleared and purified the air, and sickness and cholera disappeared for a time.

Early in July orders were received to hold the regiment in readiness to proceed in country boats to Cawnpore, and about the middle of the month all the arrangements were completed by the commissariat, and a fleet of about 80 or more boats had arrived at Chinsurah for our embarkation. The officers were granted (according to rank) a liberal money allowance to provide their own boat, and they generally got first-rate budgerows, with accommodation for two or three officers, for less than the money allowed by Government, so that the officers of each company might go together or hire a budgerow for each individually, as they liked. These boats were very comfortable, and had each two good cabins and a bath-room; and the officers' personal furniture of tables and chairs, beds, and chests of drawers left nothing wanting. All the boats were covered with canvas awnings. Each budgerow was attended by two small boats—one fitted with a clay oven and fireplace for cooking, and the other carried the luggage and servants, who kept close to their masters, and came on board without delay or difficulty whenever they were wanted. The men's boats were large, clumsy craft, with matting awnings, and calculated to accommodate from twenty to thirty soldiers, with their arms, accoutrements, and knapsacks. These had each a cooking boat attached, with cooks and assistants. There were also at least a dozen commissariat boats, with live stock and bullocks, sheep and poultry, as well as spirits and wine for the voyage, and there were hospital-boats, where none but the ailing and sick were admitted. The commissariat had also bakers' boats, so that we had fresh bread daily. Before we started each company was furnished with distinguishing flags; mine was distinct, a St. Andrew's Cross on a red ground; and in addition to the commissariat provisions, the officers had their own private stock of poultry, hams, and wines.

With all these means, good accommodation, and creature comforts one might hope for a pleasant change and merry trip on the rivers Hooghly and Ganges, but in course of this voyage we were disappointed. Notwithstanding much variety and fun, we had occasionally to encounter great difficulties. At last we got under way from Chinsurah about the end of July, with strict orders to the boats of each company to keep as much as possible together, and to be guided by their respective distinguishing flags. Any neglect of this arrangement was at once visible and checked. We had our advance and rear guards—the first an officer's budgerow, to point out any difficulties in the river to the advancing fleet, and the rear guard consisting of the captain and subaltern of the day, and one of the men's boats from each company in succession daily. Their duty was to assist any of the boats of the fleet which got into distress from accident or bad management. When the winds favoured the whole fleet made sail, and when they were against us the boats were towed along the banks of the river, or from the shallow sandbanks by the whole of the crews, by means of ropes tied to the top of the mast. This was very slow and fatiguing work against the strong currents. In this way we some days made fifteen to twenty miles, but generally not more than six.

At eight every morning the halt for breakfast was sounded, and the officers on duty selected the next favourable bank of the river for securing the boats during breakfast. To that spot all the fleet pushed on, and made fast with ropes and pegs. The Hindoo bearers and servants, on account of their religion, would not eat their food in the boats, but landed and made their sacred circle for cooking and eating on shore. Half an hour was allowed for breakfast, and the same time for dinner. At one o'clock the halt for dinner was heard, and the officers again selected a safe place. Frequent interruptions were occasioned by stress of weather, and the loss or absence of one or more boats, and we had many severe and sudden gales, which caused not only the upsetting but the total loss of several boats, and in two instances the drowning of a few unfortunate soldiers and women. At Dinapore we halted and dined with the officers of the 21st Fusiliers, and a most happy evening we had with them. We also had opportunities of visiting the principal towns on the banks of the Hooghly and Ganges, viz., Barrackpore, Dinapore, Monghyr, Patna, Benares, Ghazipore, Mirzapore, Allahabad, and several other places. At Benares we were most hospitably received and feasted by the rajah at his splendid country residence, after the English fashion. There we had also a severe gale at noonday, which carried my budgerow away from its mooring down the stream, but I managed to jump out of one of the windows up to my shoulders in the river, and fortunately got safe on shore, but of course with a good ducking. For some hours before this we dreaded a storm; the clouds were dark and heavy all the morning, and so visible was its approach that we got alarmed and landed our tents and all our baggage on the banks of the river for safety. These precautions were not long completed before the gale burst upon us with sudden fury, carrying away my budgerow and many other boats.

About this time cholera again broke out amongst our men, and we lost several, but the greater number of those attacked recovered, owing, no doubt, to our constant change of air. One supposed reason for these attacks was that in most of the confined parts of the river the floating dead and decomposed bodies of Hindoos of all ages were so numerous that they were actually massed together in hundreds where the stream drove them, and where the current was not sufficiently strong to disperse and carry them away. The Hindoos generally disposed of their dead in the holy Ganges, and consequently they were to be seen in all parts of the river and in all stages of decomposition, with vultures everywhere feeding upon them. In halting and securing our boats for the night we always selected good and firm "lagowing" ground and smooth water, and as our large fleet was packed all together, we were sure to find in the mornings dozens of these floating bodies brought up by the current, and jammed between and all round our boats in the most disgusting manner, and we could not get rid of them, nor clear of them until we were again under way and in the open running stream.

During our voyage we saw many alligators daily sunning themselves on the various sandbanks which appear in the middle and other parts of the river. They were very wild, but sometimes our sportsmen got a shot at them before they plunged into the water. Some may have been wounded, but we never knew that any had been killed. Our men were strictly forbidden to bathe, for fear of the strong currents, and of our friends the alligators, but, notwithstanding these orders, some ventured on the sly to indulge in this recreation. It was on one of these occasions that Daniel Shean,* a soldier of the light company, who was an excellent swimmer, ventured into the river, and was seen by his comrades soon after to sink, and never to rise again. The firm belief of every one was that he was seized and pulled under

* See above, p. 167.

by an alligator and carried bodily away. I omitted to mention that the officers had tiffin (lunch) at the men's dinner-hour, one o'clock, and dined after the halt of the day, generally about sunset, and enjoyed themselves afterwards till bedtime either visiting, or resting with every comfort round them, in their budgerows. At last we reached Cawnpore, in the middle of October, having been about three months on our voyage.

CHAPTER XXVIII

IN COMMAND AT CAWNPORE

Life at Cawnpore—Quarrel between Mowatt and Burke—Court-martial.

IN spite of our disasters and losses, we enjoyed ourselves fairly well. Our commissariat was perfect. In fine weather, with the wind fair, it was a novel and imposing sight to watch our large fleet under all sail with our gay flags flying. The men's barracks were ready to receive the regiment, and as we had sent on our bearers some days before to select quarters, we all found comfortable houses ready for us on our arrival. The barracks were on a rising open ground near the river. We were allowed lodging money according to rank, which was more than sufficient for the field officers to have each a large and comfortable bungalow, with many rooms, baths, and stables, and the others had similar accommodation by two or three of them joining and living together. There was also a most liberal money allowance for our mess house. The district was commanded by Major-

General Gray, and the station by Major-General Sir Joseph Thackwell, and Captain Tudor of our regiment was A.D.C. to the former. We found the 11th and 31st Regiments of Bengal Native Infantry, and several batteries of European Bengal Artillery and the 5th Bengal Native Cavalry in garrison on our arrival. The 9th Lancers joined us soon after. Nothing very remarkable occurred during the first twelve months of our residence at Cawnpore. We had frequent social gatherings at our respective messes, and our two generals entertained us repeatedly. In January, 1843, Colonel Woodhouse received the local rank of major-general and was appointed to command at Meerut, and I succeeded again to the command of the 50th Regiment.

An unfortunate quarrel took place at Cawnpore between two of our officers, Lieutenant Mowatt and Assistant-Surgeon Bourke, and a general court-martial was unavoidable, the first which was known on an officer of our regiment for thirty-nine years. They were playing billiards after dinner and differed, or rather quarrelled, when some very offensive language was used by both, but more especially by Bourke. A challenge to fight a duel followed from Mowatt, and Bourke declined to fight except with swords. The seconds objected to this, and insisted on pistols as the customary weapon with Englishmen, but Bourke remained obstinate, and would only fight with swords. Next morning they went out and met at an appointed place, the seconds, or rather Bourke's friend, being provided with both pistols and swords. Here again Bourke insisted on his right to choose his own arms. After a good deal of talk, without any effect on Bourke's decision, Mowatt said, " Well, sir, then here is at you, with swords," taking up one and putting himself in a posture of defence at the same moment. Bourke then declined to fight at all! clearly showing he never intended doing so, and that he named swords in the hope of avoiding altogether a hostile meeting. They then returned to their quarters and communicated all that happened to Captain Wilton, the senior officer present when the quarrel took place, who at once put them both under arrest and reported the whole of this most discreditable affair to me as the commanding officer. Until then I knew nothing whatever of it.

After due consideration I was satisfied that nothing less than their removal from the regiment or a general court-martial could take place, and I was unwilling for the honour of the regiment to have recourse to the latter expedient. I therefore determined to report the whole affair to Major-General Sir Joseph Thackwell, commanding the garrison, and afterwards, if necessary, to Major-General Gray, commanding the district, and to procure leave of absence for them both for the express purpose of exchanging at once to some other regiments; and in making this request to both these general officers I founded my request on the high character of the regiment and my unwillingness to stain our reputation by a general court-martial, and told them that for thirty-nine years the 50th Regiment had not had one officer brought to trial. Sir Joseph Thackwell heard me most kindly and fully entered into my feelings and wishes, and recommended me at once to see General Gray on the subject; and that officer in like manner agreed to my request, but stated that in making my application to Major-General Sir Harry Smith, the Adjutant-General of the Army, for their leave of absence, I must state the whole of the circumstances, and my unwillingness to tarnish the high reputation of my regiment by recourse to a general court-martial. To this I agreed, and made my application to the adjutant-general accordingly (my old comrade, Sir Harry Smith), which was forwarded and recommended in due course by Generals Thackwell and Gray. But by return of post I received rather a severe letter from Sir Harry Smith, informing me that if the officers named were not fit to serve in the 50th Regiment they were not fit to serve in any other, and ordering me at once to prefer written charges against them, with a view to their being immediately brought before a general court-martial.

I had now no other course left, so I sent in my charges without further delay, and, in a few days more, the general order for the court-martial appeared, to assemble at Cawnpore on a given day. That day soon arrived, and the court-martial assembled accordingly, Colonel Scott, C.B., of the 9th Lancers, being the president. As a matter of duty, I was obliged to appear as prosecutor, and the court being duly sworn and the prisoners arraigned, I was called forward. I commenced my address to the court by lamenting my present most painful and distressing duty, and yet my comparative satisfaction in being able to say that my previous intimacy and friendship with the prisoners, especially with Lieutenant Mowatt, must prove to the court, to them, and to the world that I was in no way influenced by any unkind or vindictive feeling : on the contrary, that I sincerely sympathized with them, and with the distress of every officer of the regiment on this trying occasion. I then spoke much of the high character and reputation of the regiment, the constant and great unanimity and brotherly friendship of its officers, and the absence for thirty-nine years of any such occurrence ; and concluded with an ardent hope that the present would be the first and last occasion of its kind. I then called in succession the officers who were present and witnessed the various matters stated in the charges, and the prisoners having offered nothing in their defence beyond calling on me and several of the other senior officers to speak of their previous character and conduct, the proceedings here closed, and the court was cleared to deliberate on its finding and sentence.

The proceedings were forwarded in the usual manner for the consideration of the Commander-in-Chief, General Lord Gough. I remained very anxious, for the evidence was so clear that I could not but anticipate the result, and I was especially sorry and concerned for my little friend and protégé, Lieutenant Mowatt. At last the General Orders promulgating the finding and sentence of the court arrived. Both were found guilty. Lieutenant Mowatt was sentenced to be severely reprimanded, and Assistant-Surgeon Bourke to be cashiered. These sentences were approved and confirmed by the Commander-in-Chief, but in consideration of the high character and renown of the 50th Regiment, his Excellency the Commander-in-Chief was pleased to remit both sentences and to order these officers to return to their duties. This was most gratifying to us all, for we considered this the highest compliment that could be paid to the regiment, and next we rejoiced to find our friend Mowatt (who was a general favourite) again back in safety and honour amongst us; but Dr. Bourke was not much liked at any time, and now, from his pusillanimous conduct, less than ever. Fortunately for him, his seniority in the service led to his promotion at home to be surgeon of another regiment before anything of this court-martial was known in England, and so he left us for ever soon after.

CHAPTER XXIX

THE GWALIOR CAMPAIGN

Expedition to Gwalior—In command of the regiment—Brigadier Black—His accident—I am appointed to the command of the brigade—Battle of Punniar—In General Gray's absence I order a charge on the enemy's guns—Severely wounded

SHORTLY after this we had more pleasant and exciting hopes and prospects. War—war! Rumours of war were now heard everywhere, and I soon received orders to hold the regiment in readiness for immediate service. Most of our officers were young, and, with the exception of myself, I believe not one of them had ever seen a shot fired in earnest. All our men were equally strangers to a campaign, but all were full of ardour and zeal, and most anxious to meet an enemy. As I knew them to be well in hand and in the most perfect state of discipline, I was not less proud of my command and of the prospect of showing (should the opportunity offer) that we were all equal to our duty. In a few days the General

Orders detailed the particulars of an expedition against the revolted troops of the Maharajah and government of Gwalior. Our forces were divided into two distinct bodies. The larger, consisting of many of her Majesty's regiments of infantry and cavalry and European artillery, and a number of regiments of Bengal native infantry and cavalry and artillery, with commissariat and medical departments, was concentrated from the different up-country stations, and ordered to rendezvous at a given place under the immediate command of the Commander-in-Chief, then Sir Hugh Gough, attended by the Governor-General, Lord Ellenborough, all the headquarters staff, and several general officers in command of divisions and brigades, and all these marched upon Gwalior by a given route. The second column of the army, under Major-General Gray, consisted of the 3rd Buffs, the 50th Regiment, and the 9th Lancers. Also five regiments of Bengal native infantry, two regiments of Bengal native cavalry, and several batteries of European artillery, commissariat, and medical departments marched from Cawnpore and Allahabad and other stations in November, and were concentrated for the first time in brigades on a very extensive plain about half-way between Gwalior and Cawnpore. There we halted, encamped, and remained for nearly three weeks.

Our brigade was composed of the 50th Regiment and the 50th and 58th Regiments of Native

Infantry, and under the command of Brigadier Black, of the Bengal army. That officer had for many years held a civil appointment, and candidly confessed that he knew nothing of the duties of a military command and much less of manœuvring a body of men. At this time General Gray had us out daily at brigade field-days, allowing each brigadier to select his own manœuvres. I was the second in command of our brigade, and our zealous brigadier used to come daily to my tent, and, with all simplicity and candour, confess that he really could not attempt to manœuvre his men unless I assisted him by giving him a regular lesson of what he was to do each day. I, of course, consented to do so, and wrote him out five or six simple manœuvres for each day, and explained them over and over again until he appeared to understand them perfectly. He used then to leave me and to study his lesson for the rest of the evening, and so well that, when he appeared on parade next day, from memory he put his brigade through the required movements with perfect confidence and without once making a mistake, and he continued this daily, while we remained in that encampment.

During the whole of this time we knew that the main body of our army under Sir Hugh Gough was halted and encamped within twenty miles of us, on a different road to our right, and employed daily like ourselves in field-days. Native troopers, with dispatches, passed between both divisions almost daily. I never knew the reason of this delay; but it was by many believed to be caused by awaiting the result of pending negotiations. At last we again got *en route*, our division still keeping the main road from Cawnpore to Gwalior through the Antre Pass, with orders to examine that formidable position before we attempted to enter it. While halted and encamped on the evening of the 25th December our brigadier had a serious accident. He was examining his pistols, when one of them suddenly went off and wounded him severely in the head. This obliged him to be sent at once to the rear to the nearest military station, and I was on the same day appointed by General Gray to the command of the brigade, with the rank of brigadier. Such is the fate and chance of war, and I was delighted with my promotion and prospects, for we were now more than ever certain of meeting our enemy, the Mahrattas, in battle.

But before I go further I must mention that on leaving Cawnpore I wrote to my agent, John Allan, at Calcutta, requesting him to insure my life in favour of my dear wife for £6,000, and while delayed in camp Mr. Allan sent me the necessary papers for me and our surgeon to fill up and sign, to enable him to complete the insurance. This was duly done and the papers returned to him, and by return of post I had another letter from Mr. Allan, saying all was right, that I might make myself

THE GWALIOR CAMPAIGN 233

perfectly easy. But on the very evening of my promotion as brigadier I received another letter from Mr. Allan, informing me that the insurance office (being now confident of our going into action) had declined the insurance on my life without an additional high premium, and begging to know what he was to do. I instantly wrote to him declining, and saying that I would take my chance, as I had often done before.

On the morning of the fourth day after this, namely, on the 29th of December, we came in sight of the Antre Pass, and General Gray, with a strong escort of cavalry, having been sent on to reconnoitre, soon returned at full speed to inform the Commander-in-Chief that the pass was strongly occupied by the enemy, with many guns in battery. A halt was then ordered, and after half an hour's consultation with his staff, General Gray ordered us to stand again to our arms, and put the column in motion at a right angle to our left, thus intending to turn the enemy's position, and so march upon Gwalior. Some of us felt this a disappointment, but we soon heard that the general's orders were not to attack the enemy unless he attacked us.

We commenced our flank march. There was a ridge of hills running for miles directly parallel to our route, and not many hundred yards from us. We, quite unconscious of any danger, never thought of reconnoitring that ground, which our general decidedly should have done, and continued our flank march with only the usual precautions of our advance and rear guards, and from one end to the other (with our column and baggage, commissariat, and bazaar) we must have occupied a line of road of at least ten miles. Still nothing happened, nothing was expected, until about three o'clock in the evening, when the column was halted for the day and began to prepare to receive our tents and camp equipage. Then we were suddenly roused by bang, bang of artillery in our rear, and soon after by cavalry videttes from the rear guard (still many miles from us) galloping into our lines in great confusion, and frantically shouting that our rear guard was attacked and being cut to pieces.

It was now ascertained that from the time we changed our line of march to the left, so as to turn the Antre Pass, the enemy left that position also, and moved all day parallel to our position and column, keeping the ridge of hills between us until they came over and attacked our rear guard. The "Assembly" was immediately sounded, and we stood to our arms, and reinforcements of native infantry and cavalry were instantly dispatched to assist the rear guard, and at the same time the 3rd Regiment of Buffs, under Lieut.-Colonel Cluney, was sent to the left front over a spur of the ridge of hills already mentioned, my brigade and Brigadier Wheeler's remaining stationary with the general and staff, all ready for orders. Meantime the attack and defence of the rear guard became louder and nearer, and we could hear not only constant discharges of artillery, but regular volleys of musketry and independent file firing, and with these we could distinctly hear a heavy cannonade at a considerable distance. This we supposed at the time to be from Gwalior; but it afterwards proved to be our troops under the command of our Commander-in-Chief, Sir Hugh Gough, engaged in battle with the enemy at Maharajpore.

In a very short time a staff officer came galloping back from Colonel Cluney and reported that the enemy was in great force in his front; on which General Gray ordered me to advance with my brigade to the support, with all speed. We moved off in open columns of companies at the double, and soon found ourselves under the range of the enemy's guns, fired from the other side of the ridge of hills, and the shot now passing over us. When we got close under the rising ground I halted my brigade in close columns of regiments, and the general rode up and inquired angrily why I had halted. I said to load, as I thought it was now high time to do so, for the enemy's shots were still passing rapidly over us. As soon as we had loaded, I advanced the whole brigade as we then stood, in close column of companies by regiments, and as soon as we reached the summit of the hill we came at once in sight of a large portion of the Mahratta army in order of battle, and were instantly under a heavy fire from their artillery and infantry. I rode in front of my column, and deployed them on the grenadiers of the 50th Regiment, the 50th Native Infantry taking our right and the 58th Native Infantry our left. All this was done in double quick and without the slightest confusion, and all as steady as rocks. I then took my station in rear of the centre, and ordered my bugler to sound "Commence firing." Up to that time, so admirably steady were the men that not a shot was fired until the order was given. But then they opened in earnest, and kept it up with the most steady regularity. Meantime, two batteries of our artillery were brought to our right, followed by our first infantry brigade, and these got at once into action, and about half a mile to our left we saw Colonel Cluney and his regiment and a battery of our artillery warmly engaged, and sending shots occasionally into the enemy's columns and batteries in our front.

By this time a number of our men fell killed and wounded, and it was now getting late and the sun about setting. A deep rough and rocky valley separated us from the enemy. My men were falling fast, and I saw no chance of driving our foes before us without crossing the valley and giving them the bayonet. I looked round everywhere for

THE GWALIOR CAMPAIGN 237

General Gray and his staff, but could nowhere see them. I asked my brigade-major if he knew where the general was, but he did not; so rather than lose a chance, and my men, without doing any good, I instantly made up my mind to advance and at them. I ordered my bugler to sound the "Advance." It was at once passed along the line, and off we went at a rapid, steady pace down the valley, keeping up a brisk independent firing all the while, and receiving the enemy's shot and shell and musketry in rapid succession. The ground was so rough, with loose rocks and stones, that I and all the mounted officers were obliged to dismount; but with the loss of some men killed and wounded we managed to reach a clear space at the bottom of the valley. It was then all but dark, when, after hurriedly reforming our ranks, I gave the order to charge the enemy's guns, and at this instant I positively saw one of the Mahratta artillerymen put his match to his gun (not many hundred yards from us), the contents of which (grape-shot) knocked me and Captain Cobbam and about a dozen men of my brave 50th over. Captain Hough and two or three men came instantly to assist me, and offered to take me to the rear, where the medical officers were sure to be found; but I said, " No ; never mind me: take those guns!" and with many hearty cheers they were all taken in a few minutes, the brave Mahrattas standing by their guns to the last, and refusing to quit them or to run, when positively ordered and pushed aside by our men's bayonets. Move they would not, until they were slaughtered on the spot.

When I was hit I was knocked clean over, and thought it was from a round shot, and that I was, of course, done for. My only care and regret was that my dear wife would lose the intended insurance on my life, and so be left, with our children, worse off than I intended. These thoughts occupied my mind until I was soon after assisted off the field by Sergeant Quick and two soldiers to where the medical officers were attending to the wounded. I had not got far when, by the light of the new moon, just rising, I saw an officer sitting under a tree, bleeding profusely, and resting his head on one arm, and with two or three soldiers supporting him. I inquired who it was, and was told Captain Cobbam, wounded severely in five different places, but still alive. I told them who I was, and that I was then on my way to the doctors, and begged the men to take him there also. A few yards farther on I met the surgeon of the 9th Lancers. He then examined my wound, putting one of his fingers in where the ball entered, and another where it passed out of my body, and then said, "Never fear; you are all right." This was indeed cheering, and enough to make me forget my fears about the loss to my dear wife of the insurance on my life. He then ordered my escort to take me a little way farther over the hill, where they would find all the medical officers and wounded. We reached them in safety, but faint from much loss of blood. I was again examined, dressed, and well bandaged, and again reassured and told not to be alarmed, as my wound, though severe, was not dangerous. They then put me in a doolie with four bearers and my escort, and ordered them to carry me direct to our camp.

CHAPTER XXX

WOUNDED AND MADE MUCH OF

"My brigade had carried all before it"—Painful return to camp—General Gray's dispatch

I NOW felt much refreshed, and was more pleased with my wound and my good luck than if I had altogether escaped, and, finally, I began to calculate on the honour and glory which must follow our victory, for I was told before I left the field of battle that my brigade had carried all before it. The new moon soon failed, and my escort and I were suddenly left in utter darkness, in a rough and undulating country, without a path or any other means to guide us. It was a bitter cold night, and I soon became alarmed lest we should lose our way and perhaps get into the enemy's lines, and I was not less afraid that my doolie-bearers might bolt and leave me to my sufferings for the night. In this critical situation I called to Sergeant Quick to halt for a moment, and then told him and his men to keep a sharp look out on the bearers, and if they attempted to run, to fire upon them, and, if possible, to try and explain this to them. I then told him that if he heard or saw any suspicious-looking men to let me know at once, but not to attempt to fire until I ordered. I still retained my sword in my hand, and had perfect possession of my faculties, and, if attacked, my mind was fully made up to fight for my life.

We wandered and wandered for nearly an hour without any signs of our camp, or meeting any one, or knowing where we were going. I felt the piercing cold more and more, for there was a sharp frost, and I was sensible of losing blood fast through my bandages, for my doolie was well saturated with it. I confess I felt uneasy and alarmed, and in this state I now ordered Sergeant Quick to put me down so as to rest the bearers, and himself to go a little in front and to lie down and listen for any sounds which might reach him. He soon returned and said he could hear nothing, and proposed that we should go on to the top of a rising ground not far from us. We did so, and again I was put down, and the sergeant went out in front again to listen, returning soon with the joyful news that he heard the noise of wheels, as if of artillery or wagons. I then directed them to take me up and to make for that direction. My teeth were now chattering with the cold, and I felt weaker and weaker, but we managed to get over another half-mile or more of ground, and then I was put down once more, and the sergeant, as before, went to listen. He now returned in all haste, saying he could see numerous lights and was sure it was our own camp! This truly revived and cheered us all, and off we started almost at a trot, and, sure enough, in half an hour more we entered our camp, and soon after I was in my own tent and my own bed.

I was indeed thankful, but so cold and shivering that I asked a native hospital assistant, who soon found me, if a glass of hot brandy and water would do me any harm. He said not the least, so I immediately sent my kitmutgar to our mess-man to get one for me; it was brought, and I did enjoy it, and was just finishing the last drop, when in came our surgeon, Dr. Davidson, and on being told what I had done he instantly pitched into his hospital assistant, and in real anger threatened to destroy him, for giving me the means of causing inflammation and fever! When he got a little cool he removed my bandages, dressed my wounds, and again wrapped me up securely for the night, and put me to bed, leaving strict orders with my bearer and kitmutgar to remain with me, to give me nothing but barley-water if I wanted a drink, and to call him if necessary. I soon became warm and composed, and upon the whole had a good and quiet night, and slept at intervals soundly. Next morning Dr. Davidson examined and dressed my wound, and told me I had had a narrow escape, and that I was now doing well. He also informed me that poor Cobbam was dead; he had received no less than five grape-shot, three in his body and two in his arm, and died in a doolie soon after I saw him.

My wound was about three inches above the left groin, close to the hip, and happily without touching the bone; had it been one inch more to the right it would have been fatal, and instant death, but it pleased God to order otherwise, and I was then, and continue to this day, truly thankful. I said before, I was knocked clean over, and thought it was by a round shot. It struck me on the waist-belt, carrying parts of my belt, trousers, drawers, shirt, and flannel in with it, and the getting rid of these fragments day after day in threads and small particles afterwards caused me more pain than any sufferings from my wound. These grape-shots were made up in a canvas bag as large as the body of a bottle, with wooden bottoms, and tied at the top with strong cord. They contained from eighty to a hundred jagged balls, nearly twice the size of an ordinary musket-ball, and they were secured by cords wound crossways and about an inch apart on the bag. When discharged or fired the bag is burst at once, and the balls carry death and destruction, broadcast, wherever they fall. My belt being shot through, it dropped off, and with it I lost my scabbard, which I regretted then, and do to this day.

So ended in victory the battle of Punniar, on the night of the 29th of December, 1843. All the enemy's guns were taken, and the survivors of their army fled in utter confusion and disorder, leaving all their baggage and stores and many arms behind. Strange to say, on the same day the main body of the Mahratta army was similarly defeated by Sir Hugh Gough and our headquarters forces at Maharajpore. This was the distant cannonade and firing which we heard before going into action.

For a day or two the doctor would not allow any one to see me, but soon after I had many visits from my brother-officers, and all to congratulate me on my escape, and, above all, on what they were pleased to call my "daring, dashing charge across the valley." Every one spoke of this, and said it had decidedly crowned the success of the day.

At last General Gray's dispatch appeared in the public papers, and after detailing at length the operations of the day, he concluded by saying that "the 2nd Infantry Brigade, under Brigadier Anderson, of H.M. 50th Regiment, by an able and judicious movement turned the enemy's position, charged and took his guns, and so contributed to the final success of the day." My officers were not even satisfied with this, and maintained that much more should have been said, and all blamed Captain Tudor, the A.D.C., who was known to have great influence with the general and to have had much to say and to do in writing the official report of the battle. In short, Tudor was everything with the general, even to the management of his household, and for this he was familiarly and privately called "the chief butler," and during an angry discussion of this dispatch, our paymaster, Captain Dodd (who was a witty fellow), summed up by saying, "Yes, yes; the chief butler forgot Joseph!" It was also urged and maintained that, supposing I had failed in my dash into the valley and lost my brigade or been defeated, General Gray would then have blamed me for attempting to move without his orders, and perhaps brought me to a general court-martial. But all is well that ends well, and so I am satisfied, although I do confess I was, like my friends, a little disappointed at the time.

We remained some days in our encampment at Punniar, and then marched for Gwalior, where we found the rest of our field forces encamped under the Commander-in-Chief, Sir Hugh Gough. The Governor-General, Lord Ellenborough, and his numerous staff were also encamped with our army. Here we continued for nearly three weeks, during which time the most happy and social intercourse took place between the different regiments and corps. We all had our splendid mess marquees and full establishments, wines and luxuries of every kind, and nothing wanting, and public dinners every day followed as a matter of course. The Governor-General and Sir Hugh Gough had also their magnificent establishments, and had their tables crowded every day with guests from each of the regiments. I and many others were confined to our tents and to our beds from our wounds, and could not share in these festivities, but whatever was ordered and good for us we received regularly from our respective messes.

I had another advantage: my tent was pitched so near our mess marquee that I could almost distinctly hear every word that was spoken, and frequently my own name and health drunk with much cheering and applause. This acknowledgment may sound to others like vanity, but I still confess I was well pleased and proud of the good opinion of my brother-warriors.

CHAPTER XXXI

RETURN TO CAWNPORE

Slow recovery from my wound—Painful journey by palanquin to Cawnpore—Am created a C.B.—Other honours and promotions

THE weather still continued bitterly cold, and about daylight on one of these mornings a tall figure, more than usually wrapped, entered my tent, stood in the door, and asked kindly, "How are you getting on, colonel?" I must have been in pain or bad humour, for I bluntly said, "Who are you—what do you want?" He quietly answered, "Lord Ellenborough," so I at once asked a thousand pardons and begged he would walk in and sit down. He continued his inquiries most kindly, and took a chair and sat down by my bedside. He remained some time with me, and paid me many more visits afterwards. He was also in the habit of visiting all the other wounded officers and men daily, and to the latter (in bad cases) he used to give gold mohurs to comfort them for their sufferings, and these our men prized very much and made into rings in remembrance of our good and popular Governor-General, Lord Ellenborough.

After these battles the Mahratta army submitted to our Government, and in about a fortnight afterwards six or eight thousand of them actually volunteered to enter our service, and were at once formed into ten regiments under British officers selected from the Bengal native forces, and styled from that day " The Gwalior Contingent." They remained faithful to our service until the general mutiny of the native Bengal army, and then I believe they joined the revolt to a man.

About this time I had the happiness of receiving more than one letter from my dear wife, and I made many efforts on my back and in my bed to write to her. My first letter was written a few days after I was wounded, and I managed to get my sash across my back under my arms, and tied to that a piece of rope, secured and tightened to the top of the pole of my tent, so as to raise and support my head and upper part of my body, and so enable me to write pretty comfortably. I was in high spirits, and I gave her a cheering account of my sufferings and a glowing report of my success.

Our encampment was outside the town and fort of Gwalior, and our officers made frequent visits to both, and especially to the fort, which was very extensive and well worth seeing. It is built upon a long and very high range of rocks, and only accessible by one entrance over a drawbridge, the road to which is a long and narrow one, over a minor spur of the same chain of rocks. I was curious to see this formidable fortification, and on one fine morning I was raised from my bed and put into a doolie, well propped up with pillows by my good and trusty friend Captain Dodd. He and a few more of the officers accompanied me on my excursion. The change and fresh air did me great good, and I was much pleased with all I saw, and with the marked and courteous civilities we received from the Mahratta officers and soldiers who garrisoned the fort, for at this time all enmity between us had passed away, and our officers and men were in the habit of meeting them daily and constantly.

I do not remember anything more of any particular note taking place while our army remained before Gwalior. About the last week in January, General Orders were issued for the whole of our forces to return to their former respective quarters, and my regiment commenced its march soon after for Cawnpore. After I was wounded I gave up the immediate command of my regiment to Major Petit, leaving all the daily details to him; but he consulted me in all important matters, and always fixed the hours of marching in the mornings at the time most convenient to me. I was carried in my doolie at the head

of my regiment every day, and on halting found
my tent all ready pitched in proper position, with
my bed and all my comforts prepared for me; for
in returning to Cawnpore through a free country
our baggage, commissariat, and stores always took
the advance of our column of march, and arrived
on our camping-ground each morning some time
before us. Such was the efficiency of our native
servants that everything, even to our breakfasts,
was ready on our arrival. Our march seldom
exceeded from ten to fifteen miles daily, so that
we were comfortably camped and settled before
the heat became oppressive, and the remainder
of each day was spent by the officers and men
as they best could. I continued to get on as
well as could be expected, but as I could only
lie in one position (on my right side), my arm,
shoulder, and hip became sore and chafed, and
this and the jolting of my doolie, and latterly
of my palanquin, left me much fatigued each day
before our march was over. In this way our
daily journey was continued for three weeks, a
distance of two hundred and twenty miles to
Cawnpore, and there we arrived at last in safety,
about the middle of February. I marched in, or
rather was carried in, at the head of my regiment,
in my palanquin, with our band playing "See
the Conquering Hero comes." All the women
and children and the few troops and invalids
who remained in garrison turned out to receive

and welcome us, and the cheering and shouting which followed, and the welcomes, and "God save the Colonel!" from one and all, were, I confess, most gratifying to me.

We were soon comfortably settled in our old quarters. I was obliged to keep my bed for some months afterwards, but continued otherwise in good health and spirits, and my medical friends assured me I was progressing as well as they could wish. My greatest sufferings were from the constant and unchanged position on my right side to which I was obliged to keep, and from the still continued extraction of threads and small particles of clothing which had been carried into my wound. But at last this painful annoyance ceased, and from that time healing followed rapidly.

In March we received official acknowledgment of our services from the Home authorities, with notices of various honours and promotions conferred in consequence. I had the proud satisfaction of seeing my name amongst the few who were appointed by her Majesty to be Companions of the Bath. My friends Majors Ryan and Petit were made brevet lieut.-colonels, and Major-General Gray a K.C.B., and his A.D.C., Captain Tudor (the chief butler), a brevet major. All other officers of both divisions of our army who had similar claims were either decorated or promoted. I had also the satisfaction of receiving a letter from our agents, Messrs. Cox & Co., informing me that the Secretary of War had been pleased to grant me eighteen months' additional pay for my wounds (commonly called "blood money"), and authorizing me to draw for the same. We were further informed that her Majesty the Queen was graciously pleased to order that the regiments engaged at Maharajpore should bear the name on their colours and appointments, and the regiments engaged at Punniar, that name in like manner on their colours and appointments. All this good news was very cheering and gratifying to us, and all expressed their readiness to fight and to conquer again. Then followed an order from the Governor-General of India granting to each officer and soldier who served in either of these battles a decoration, a bronze star to be worn on the left breast, suspended from the ribbon of India, and to be made from the cannon captured in these actions, with the words "Maharajpore, 29th December, 1843," on a silver medallion on the centre of the star, for the troops who served there; the word "Punniar," with the same date, for those who fought and conquered at that place; and soon after this I had the honour of receiving mine (one of the first cast), with a kind and flattering letter from Lord Ellenborough.

CHAPTER XXXII

ON LEAVE FOR TWO YEARS

Riding accident at Cawnpore—Foot seriously injured—Get two years' leave of absence—Voyage to Cape Town—On to Australia—A strange cabin

ABOUT three months after our return to Cawnpore I was able to move about a little on crutches, but not to go to parades for some months more, nor to sleep nor rest on my left side. At last I managed to resume the command of the regiment and to carry on the orderly room duties, and finally to attend parades mounted; but I could not carry my sword, although my wound was by this time quite healed up, for the parts were so tender and sensitive that I could not bear the weight and friction of my sword against my side. My orderly, therefore, always carried it for me. On the very first ride I attempted to take into the country, my horse shied while passing a bullock-dray on a small, low bridge (not more than three or four feet high), slipping his hind legs over the bridge and falling backwards right over with me. We both came down together, and my right foot stuck in the stirrup, until the weight of my body carried it clear away. My ankle was much sprained in consequence, but I got up at once and managed, with the assistance of two officers who were with me, to mount again and to ride home. I sent at once for our surgeon, who ordered me to keep quiet and to bathe my ankle constantly in cold water under a pump. For days and weeks I thought very little of my accident, but my ankle and leg swelled very much and got worse and worse, with much pain, for many months afterwards. Various lotions were applied, but I got no better, and as my general health now began to fail, I was frequently confined to bed for weeks, and almost to the house for twelve months.

I now seriously began to think of getting leave of absence, and in December of this year (1844) I consulted our surgeon, Dr. Davidson, accordingly, and he said there would be no difficulty in granting my request. So he at once wrote an official letter recommending me for leave of absence to proceed to Calcutta for the purpose of appearing before a medical board, and that letter I myself (as commanding officer) forwarded to the Adjutant-General of H.M. Forces in India for the consideration of the Commander-in-Chief, and in the next General Orders my name appeared for leave to Calcutta for the purpose above stated.

In January, 1845, I took public leave of the

ON LEAVE FOR TWO YEARS

officers of my regiment in the mess-room, and with Captain Waddy (who also got leave of absence), Mrs. Waddy, and their children, left Cawnpore for Calcutta. We travelled together as far as Benares. There I took passage in one of the well-found and comfortable public river steamers, but Captain Waddy and family hired a budgerow and soon followed with the current, but did not reach Calcutta till a fortnight after us. I had previously written to my friend and agent, John Allan (one of the wealthy merchants of the "City of Palaces"), telling him that he might expect me, and requesting him to make every inquiry for passages for us to Sydney or to any part of Australia. He received me most kindly, and insisted on my taking up my quarters under his hospitable roof. He told me there was no chance of a direct passage to Australia, but that he had written to Mauritius and to Singapore to inquire if we could get passages in a vessel from either of these places for our destination.

Meantime I reported my arrival to the military authorities, and was told a medical board would assemble on a given day, and that I had better call on Dr. Murray, Inspector of Hospitals and chief of the Medical Department. I did so, and after a conversation, in which I expressed my wish to be sent to Sydney, where my family then was, he said he was afraid he could not recommend me to be sent there, as his instructions were to send officers who received long sick-leave direct to England. I explained that that would not suit me at all, as to see my wife and family was of more importance to me than even my health. He then said he would consider it and would give me an answer the next day. I called the following morning, and he told me that in the event of my medical board recommending me for leave of absence, he would request I might be sent to Sydney. A few days afterwards I appeared before the board, and after they had asked me a few questions my leave was granted for two years, to proceed to New South Wales for the recovery of my health.

By this time Mr. Allan had received answers to his letters to Singapore and to Mauritius informing him there was not the slightest chance of finding passages from either of those places to Australia; he therefore advised me to go at once to the Cape of Good Hope, where we would be sure to find vessels for Sydney, as many of the English traders for that port called at the Cape for supplies. A fine ship was ready to sail in a few days for England, touching at Mauritius and at the Cape, so the Waddys and I secured our passages at once, with the understanding that we might leave either at Port Louis or at Table Bay, but when we arrived at the former there was no prospect of a passage for any port of Australia, so we proceeded in a few days to Cape Town. There we landed and took up our quarters at a most excellent lodging-house; with us were two officers of the Madras army, one of whom was a medical man, well acquainted with my late brother, and he was most kind and useful to me. We were there for a week or ten days, and there being still no hope of a passage, we all made up our minds to leave our lodgings and to go together and occupy a very nice and partly furnished house in the country, five miles from Cape Town.

There we lived comfortably for another ten days, when Captain Waddy returned in a great hurry from the town one day to tell us that the ship *Penyard Park* had just arrived, bound for Sydney; she had put in for supplies, but was so full that he was afraid we should have some difficulty in getting passages. We at once determined to take our chances, no matter how limited the accommodation. Captain Waddy started, intending to go on board and to secure, at any price, the best cabins he could get for us. In a few hours he was back, and told us he had had much difficulty in securing for us two cabins at exorbitant prices— one cabin for himself and family on the lower deck, with scarcely any light or air, and for me, the second mate's cabin, of only five feet long and four feet wide, leading from the quarter-deck into the poop, and where it was impossible for me in any way to stretch myself or lie down at full length. For this I was asked to pay seventy pounds, while Captain Waddy was to pay eighty for his. But we could not help it, and Captain and Mrs. Waddy made up their minds to go at any price, and to put up with any inconvenience, rather than lose the chance and remain behind, uncertain as to when another opportunity might offer, and for the same reasons I decided to accompany them. The captain, Sam Weller, came on shore to receive our money, and not one farthing less would he take.

The passengers were a poor and humble set. The food was indifferent, but the captain was a most attentive and first-rate seaman, and was never absent from his deck when his services were required. We sailed from the Cape about the end of April. My first night on board the *Penyard Park* was very miserable. I am six feet two inches, and could not stretch my legs, and was obliged to lie all doubled up in a most intensely uncomfortable position. I could not help complaining next morning. The captain said he was very sorry, but could not help me. At last a good-natured doctor said, " Well, Colonel Anderson, I'll see if I can help you." He then consulted his wife, and soon returned to say that, as his cabin was next to mine, he would order the carpenter to cut a hole through the partition above the level of his bed and raise my bed to that height, then to place over him a box long enough to receive my legs, and thus lengthen my bed as much as necessary. This novel mode of accommodation was soon completed by the carpenter, and from that day I was comparatively comfortable in my little cabin, and more than glad to hear that, although my box and my extra length were over the good doctor's legs every night during the voyage, he felt no inconvenience from the intrusion.

CHAPTER XXXIII

AUSTRALIA ONCE MORE

Sydney once more—Visit Mangalore—Select land for house near Melbourne—My War Medal

AFTER a rather long and stormy passage we reached Sydney on the 4th June. An old servant of mine came on board at once, and from him I heard that my dear wife and children were all quite well and at Parramatta, so I at once wrote to her to announce my arrival, and promised to be with them in course of the day. I then hurried on shore and found a steamer starting for my home. There were many passengers on board who recognized me and who knew my wife, and from them I had the most delightful and cheering accounts of my family. Two anxious hours took us to Parramatta, and as we approached the wharf my house was pointed out to me on the opposite side of the river, and also my dear wife and children hurrying down to the bank to meet me, and my son Acland was seen by some of the passengers on the wharf waiting to greet me.

When he was pointed out to me I said, "Quite impossible—that cannot be my boy!" but before I had time to say another word he made a run, and a spring on to our deck, and in an instant was in my arms. My joy and delight were so great that for some seconds I could not speak. He was so grown, so handsome, well, and cheerful. It will be remembered I left him on his bed of sickness, most alarmingly ill; it was doubtful, indeed, if I should ever see him again. He then pointed out his mother and sisters anxiously waiting for us, so off we hurried. Our meeting was full of joy and thanksgiving. With the exception of my eldest daughter, Mary, I did not know one of them. So changed were they during the four years of my absence, that had I met them anywhere else I could not in any way have recognized them.

We went home and talked and talked, for we had much to say and no end of inquiries to make. Days and days passed before we became regularly composed and quietly settled down. I spent nearly a year with my wife and children, going occasionally to Sydney for a change, and to attend public and private parties and to dine at Government House. In December of that year my wife accompanied me in a steamer from Sydney to Melbourne for the purpose of visiting our station on the Goulburn River and determining whether it was advisable to settle down permanently in or near Melbourne. My health had by this time greatly improved, and I was getting over my lameness. The long sea journey from Calcutta had done me much good, and I became stronger daily. We started from Melbourne in a gig for our station, Mangalore, and after four days' easy travelling got there early in January, 1846. My nephew, William Anderson, was then in charge. When we arrived there was no better accommodation than a common bark hut, with similar places at a little distance for the men; but the weather being fine and dry, we thought we could manage for a short time. My nephew did all he could to make us comfortable, and with our daily fresh meat and vegetables we fared very well. We took several drives in different parts of the station, and in a fortnight began our return journey to Melbourne. On our arrival there we took lodgings in Queen Street, intending to remain for some time and, if possible, to select some ground for our future residence.

Our inquiries for ground led me to make the acquaintance of a Mr. Archibald MacLaughlin, a wealthy merchant of Melbourne, who took us one morning to look at the land and site upon which my happy home, "Fairlie House," now stands, the adjoining land having been previously purchased by himself. The situation we at once thought beautiful, though then rough and without any house near it, or any signs or traces of the fine roads, streets, and houses which are now so near and all around it. However, after due consideration and visiting many other localities, I made up my mind to wait on his Honour Mr. La Trobe and request I might be allowed a special sale by auction of the land; he was the superintendent of the Port Phillip district, and subsequently lieutenant-governor of our colony of Victoria. He received me very kindly, but said at once that he could not grant my request; that it was quite impossible that he could do so. I then spoke of my claims on the Government as an old officer and as the late superintendent for many years at Norfolk Island, but all to no purpose. He said he could not do it, and that he could make no distinction. I now remembered I had a letter from Mr. Deas Thompson, the Colonial Secretary at Sydney, expressing the readiness of the governor, Sir George Gipps, to assist me in every way in getting land in the Port Phillip district, as he understood I had thought of removing my family there. He read it, and, turning round, said with a smile, "Oh, this alters the question; I shall be glad to grant you a special sale by auction. Send me your application and name a day."

With this assurance I returned to my wife, and we agreed (as we had to return to Sydney) to leave all to Mr. MacLaughlin, and request him, as my agent, to send in the application and name a day for the sale. He kindly consented to do all this, and if successful at the sale to draw upon me for the amount. In a few days we left in the *Shamrock* steamer for Sydney, and after a pleasant passage were soon again with our children at Parramatta.

The next mail from England brought me my Order of the Bath and the long-expected War Medal with the four clasps for Maida, Talavera, Busaco, and Fuentes d'Onoro. This last gratifying distinction was for many long years objected to and opposed by the Duke of Wellington, but as often urged and recommended as a right and just acknowledgment by his late Royal Highness the Duke of York, and also by many peers and persons of distinction, for services in all parts of the world by the British army during the previous half-century. It was not till the year 1844 that the late Duke of Richmond brought the subject before the House of Lords, and, on his Grace's able showing, his motion was carried by a large majority, who recommended her Majesty to be pleased to grant to each regiment and corps her royal permission to bear on their colours and appointments the name of any victory in which they had been engaged since 1793, and for the officers and men to wear a silver medal suspended from a red ribbon with blue edge, and clasp thereon for every battle or action, showing the name of every such victory. The officers of the army were so grateful to the Duke of Richmond for this service that committees were formed in London and in many of our principal towns in England, and in all foreign stations, for the purpose of getting up a subscription for a suitable testimonial in plate for his Grace, as a humble acknowledgment from the officers of the British army of the gratifying and very acceptable services he had rendered them. A large sum was collected, and a service of plate purchased and presented.

My next good news was a letter from Mr. MacLaughlin stating that at the auction he had most fortunately been able to secure for me the land I had selected. We were indeed glad, as its position is delightful—overlooking the Botanical Gardens and the Government House domain, and with exquisite views of the bay on one side, and of Richmond, Kew, and the distant hills on the other. I at once wrote to my brother, who was in London, to send me the framework of a wooden house, on the plan of the Norfolk Island Government House, which he used to admire.

CHAPTER XXXIV

SECOND VOYAGE TO CALCUTTA

Sail for India—Dangers of Torres Straits—Copang—Arrival at Calcutta—My son appointed to the 50th Regiment

THE period of my leave of absence was now drawing to a close. We received accounts from India of the campaign on the Sutlej and of the additional glory acquired by my gallant regiment in the battles of Moodkee, Ferozeshah, Aliwal, and Sobraon, and of all my dear friends who suffered or fell in those engagements. This made me more than ever anxious to be back with my regiment. In July of this year (1848) Captain Waddy and I made up our minds to take advantage of the first opportunity to secure our passages to India; soon afterwards we heard that the ship *Mary Ann* would sail for Calcutta in a few days with horses, and Captain Waddy engaged to make the necessary inquiries to secure our passages. In the meantime, after consulting with my wife and my son Acland (now in his sixteenth year), I determined to apply by

SECOND VOYAGE TO CALCUTTA 267

memorial to the Commander-in-Chief at the Horse Guards for an ensigncy for my son. Captain Waddy secured our passages, and got himself appointed to take charge of the horses, with, of course, a number of grooms under him; by this he got free passages for himself and wife, and I believe the same allowance in money which any other person so employed would have received.

I took leave of my dear wife and children on the 6th August. I slept that night at the house of my cousin, Colonel James Gordon, who was then commanding the Royal Engineers in Sydney, and embarked next day on the *Mary Ann*. We sailed for our destination, steering for the inward passage through Torres Straits. The weather was moderate and clear for the first ten days, and by this time we had passed Cape York and got well into the straits. The mainland at a distance and numerous small and large islands and rocks were constantly in sight, many of them very near. The wind was now fair, the captain and two men were constantly stationed on the fore top-sail yard, the former calling out to the men at the wheel "Port, starboard" or "Breakers ahead" or "Rocks on the lee bow" or "Port, starboard, steady!" and these were the constant warnings, almost every minute, daily. The lead was also kept going and the soundings reported, and at times a perfect silence ordered.

For days the navigation was most intricate. On one occasion we saw the masts of a schooner over a point of land; we steered round for her, and came to anchor near her. The captain asked me if I would accompany him in his boat to board her; I did so, and was a little surprised, after exchanging salutations, to find myself addressed by name by the captain, who said, "I hope Master Acland is quite well now." He told me he was from Sydney, and that my two dear boys were lodging with him when they were taken ill. This of course made me glad to meet him, to renew my thanks for his kindness to them. He was employed in the straits with his schooner, fishing for *bêche-de-mer* (or sea slugs) for the Chinese market. We left that anchorage the next morning, and after some hours' pleasant sailing got so near the mainland that we could see numbers of natives, who made signs to us, and we returned their salutation.

After this the weather got thick, with constant light rain for two or three days, and our progress became more perilous, and at times alarmingly dangerous. We could not see a hundred yards before us, and the captain had to depend entirely on his charts. On one of these trying days we reached a small island some hours before dark, and our captain prepared to bring up and anchor under the lee of it, but on getting there he could not find soundings. We then tried to get round as far as the wind would permit, but still found no bottom. He was obliged to give up all hope of coming to anchor, and could only carry on his course in the direction of the next island on his chart. He was visibly anxious, and so were we all, heavy rain still continuing and the night being unusually dark. It was indeed a black and dreadful night, and one of the most alarming I ever passed. We all kept on deck, no one went to bed, and I must confess I was afraid of going below, for I thought that if the worst happened we had a better chance of saving ourselves in the boats from the deck than if we remained below. At about two next morning the captain thought he had run a sufficient distance to be pretty near the island for which he was steering, and he therefore brought the ship to the wind, intending to lie off till daylight. This was still an anxious time, for we had yet to wait some hours. At last the day dawned, and he found himself within a few miles of the island, at the very spot he believed himself to be in, and with the appearance of better weather, the rain and fog having cleared away.

We were indeed thankful, and soon forgot our troubles, for in two hours more we were seated at a good breakfast, as merry as ever, and our ship again on her course, running away from our island, with the sun shining once more brightly on us. In another week we arrived off Booby

Island, the northern extremity of Torres Straits, thankful indeed for having got safely through that perilous voyage. The captain and Captain Waddy went on shore to the little island, taking with them, according to custom, a cask of water, a cask of salt beef, and a bag of biscuits; these were deposited in a cave in the rock called the "Post Office." It had been customary for years, for most vessels passing through the straits in safety, to leave some provisions at Booby Island, as a certain store and supply for shipwrecked sufferers, and, with humane feeling, this depot is always respected by visitors. It is named the "Post Office," as there is a large seaman's box there for letters, and also a book to insert the names of any vessels passing through, and the particulars of any losses or disasters occurring in the straits. Other ships passing take up these letters for delivery, according to their destination. Our people left letters at Booby Island, but one from me to my dear wife never reached her. She was more fortunate eighteen months later in receiving a letter left by our son Acland on his way to India.

I hope I shall never again go through Torres Straits, for it is not only a dangerous passage, but one which keeps one in constant alarm for three weeks or more. Some of the rocks seen in the direct course are not larger than a man's head over the water, others increasing to various sizes, and from the glare and rays of the sun, which are right ahead, they are not seen till one is within a few yards of them.

I have myself heard of several ships being wrecked going through the straits, and of one case where the whole of the passengers and crew fell into the hands of the natives, and were barbarously murdered and eaten, with the exception of one little boy, the son of a Captain and Mrs. D'Oyley —both of whom the unhappy child saw sacrificed with the others. He was rescued many months afterwards by Captain Lewis, of the colonial schooner *Isabella*, sent in search of the survivors by the Governor of New South Wales when news arrived in Sydney that the ship had never reached India, her destination. After many weeks' search amongst the islands, Captain Lewis got positive information from other natives that the ship was wrecked, and all on board, with the exception of one child, were murdered. He then made presents to these people, and got some of them to accompany him to the island where the massacre took place ; there, through the efforts of his new friends and allies, he was kindly received, and after many more presents the boy was delivered up to him. He was also allowed to collect and carry away all the bones he could find of the unfortunate victims. These he brought to Sydney, where they were all buried together and a handsome monument placed over them. Captain Lewis was allowed to take the survivor, little D'Oyley, home to England, to his nearest known relative; this he did at considerable inconvenience and expense. He soon discovered the grandfather, and delivered the boy to him, but instead of being handsomely rewarded for his services, he received nothing beyond expressions of many thanks, and as Captain Lewis was a poor man, depending entirely on his profession, all who knew him and this sad story were indignant, the more so as the boy's grandfather was known to be a man of considerable property.

Our detention at Booby Island was not long. We soon entered the Indian Ocean, and were steering for Copang, the capital of the Dutch island of Timor, and in three days we were safely anchored there. Our object was to fill water-casks for our horses, the consumption of water being great. Copang is an extensive, straggling, clean town, with a small fort and garrison of Dutch troops and a governor. For watering ships it is most convenient, the anchorage being within a few hundred yards of the shore, and the pure fresh water is carried in pipes to within a few yards of the beach and boats. We visited the governor and officers in the fort, who received us most kindly, and gave us coffee and cigars. We also spent many hours daily in a large shop or store, where all kinds of supplies could be purchased, and where the fat jolly Dutchman who kept it constantly treated us to coffee.

SECOND VOYAGE TO CALCUTTA 273

In a few days our tanks were full and all ready for sea, so we steered for the Bay of Bengal. The weather continued fine, and nothing remarkable occurred till our arrival off the Sand Heads. Then we received a pilot for Calcutta from one of the beautiful pilot-brigs which are constantly cruising off and on there. All was now excitement, getting scraps of news and preparing for the end of our long journey. We arrived about the middle of October, after a voyage of three months. I had the satisfaction of receiving a packet of letters from my friend John Allan, inviting me to come at once to his house, and with the gratifying news that my boy Acland was appointed to an ensigncy in my own regiment, also that the 50th was then on its march from the upper Provinces, and actually under orders for England. All these unexpected changes were in consequence of the end of our war with the Sikhs. I landed the same evening, and was hospitably received by Mr. and Mrs. Allan.

CHAPTER XXXV

TO CAWNPORE AND BACK

Violent gale at Loodhiana—Two hundred men, women, and children buried—By river steamer to Allahabad—Rejoin the regiment at Cawnpore—Return voyage down the Ganges

NEXT day I reported my arrival to the adjutant-general, to the officer commanding at Calcutta, and officially to the officer commanding the 50th Regiment. I was next agreeably surprised by a visit from one of the officers, Major Tew, who informed me that Colonel Woodhouse was on his way down, and would soon be in Calcutta, and that they were both going to England on sick-leave. He gave me much interesting news of the regiment, and from him I heard for the first time of a regrettable incident which occurred before they left Loodhiana on their present march to Calcutta. The regiment was quartered there when the Sutlej campaign commenced, and was suddenly ordered to join the army in the field at half an hour's notice. The officers were actually at their mess table when the order arrived, and they and their men were obliged to move at once, leaving the whole of their property, public and private, behind them, in charge of a guard; also the women and children and a few servants were left. The regiment was not gone many days when a large body of Sikhs marched into the town and to the military cantonments, and plundered, burnt, and destroyed almost everything there, not even sparing the officers' bungalows, many of which they either pulled down or burnt; and as they had no relish for the mess wines, they actually broke many dozens of full bottles. When the war was over the regiment returned to Loodhiana, and all were then apprised of their losses, which put them to serious inconvenience. They had not long returned before they were visited by a most violent gale, which in a few minutes levelled the men's barracks to the ground—a terrible calamity, as it buried beneath the ruins two hundred men, women, and children. About fifty of these were got out dead, the others more or less seriously wounded. To see so many brave soldiers, who had fought and escaped during the whole campaign, thus cruelly sacrificed was indeed truly heart-breaking.

I remained with my friend John Allan for more than a month. During that time I had many letters from the regiment, which kept me so well informed of their movements and march towards Calcutta that I saw no necessity to hurry my departure to meet them. An opportunity now offered direct for Sydney, and I gladly availed myself of it to write to my dear wife announcing my safe arrival. It was now the end of November, and finding that the regiment could not reach Calcutta before the beginning of March, I determined to join wherever I could most conveniently meet them on their march, and with this view took my passage early in December in one of the large and most comfortable river steamers for Allahabad. We were full of passengers for the upper Provinces, many of whom were very nice and agreeable. Our voyage up the Hooghly and Ganges lasted upwards of a month. We often stopped for some hours at the principal towns and stations to land cargo and passengers, to coal, and to receive more goods and other passengers for the higher stations. The weather was beautiful, and I enjoyed the trip and the pleasant society very much. While we were at Dinapore another of the same steamers touched there, bound for Calcutta, and in her I had the pleasure of meeting Colonel Woodhouse on his way to England. He was not in good health. Of course we had much to say during our short interview. It was not till the 7th of January that we reached Allahabad, and there we all parted, after a very agreeable voyage.

I remained a few days at the hotel, and there found my old friends Sir Harry and Lady Smith, also on their way to England. I started in a small gharrie for Cawnpore, and there took quarters at an hotel, having heard that my regiment would arrive in two days more. On the following day the adjutant, Lieutenant Mullen, and Lieutenant Mowatt came in advance to welcome me, and to escort me to the regiment, and the next day we rode out to meet it. We had not proceeded more than three miles when we saw them approaching, and as soon as they recognized me they gave three cheers, and the band struck up " John Anderson, my joe." I took off my cap and returned their greeting with a fond and grateful heart, and again, as soon as I had reached the head of the column, three more cheers saluted me. Then Colonel Petit halted the regiment, to give me the opportunity of seeing and shaking hands with all the officers, and saying a few words to the men.

We now again got *en route*, and were met by Colonel Deare and many officers of the 21st Regiment and their band, who came from Cawnpore to welcome us, and so, surrounded by many hundreds of spectators, civil and military, we reached our camping-ground. No sooner had the Fusilier band taken up its position at our head than it struck up " See the Conquering Hero comes." Colonel Deare and his officers asked us to dinner, and the men of the 21st had our men in like manner to a general and merry feast. There was no end to our toasts and our fun. Colonel Petit handed me over the command of the regiment by a written order of that day. We continued our march the following morning, and in four days reached Benares, where we found a fleet of boats ready to receive us for Calcutta. I also found letters at the post-office, leaving to me the option of taking the passage from the Ganges to the Hooghly, or, if not practicable, to proceed through the more lengthy and tedious passage of the Sunderbunds (which are the numerous outlets of the mighty Ganges to the sea), from one of which there is a canal to the Hooghly at Calcutta.

We remained two or three days encamped near Benares, making our preparations and purchasing our private stock and provisions for the voyage. The commissariat having provided amply for our men, and all being ready, we started. The weather was fine, and all went on well till we arrived off the entrance of the Hooghly from the Ganges; there we brought up, and sent boats to see, and to sound, if there was a sufficient depth of water over the bar to carry our largest boats. They returned in a few hours, and reported that there was not sufficient water, and that we must take the passage through the Sunderbunds. Next morning we started and steered accordingly, and brought up at the little village of Calpee, where it is the rule to take in pilots and provisions, and a sufficient quantity of fresh water to carry one through the Sunderbunds, as the water there is brackish half the way, and altogether salt afterwards. We found a resident magistrate at Calpee, and he furnished us at once with three pilots, and most kindly assisted us in getting provisions and many dozens of large earthen jars of fresh water. Being thus provided with a sufficient supply of all things needful for three or four weeks, we again proceeded on our voyage. One of the pilots was stationed with the advance guard, one with me as the commanding officer in the centre, and the third with the rear guard. All the boats of our fleet had strict orders to keep as much together as possible and not to lose sight of each other for a moment. As I said before, there are numerous and endless twists and turns, separate outlets and channels, in the Sunderbunds, and to take a wrong one is to take a risk of being lost altogether, and in a position from which one cannot extricate oneself to find the way back again to the proper course. To make sure, therefore, our best pilot was with the advance guard, and whenever he came to a fresh channel he halted till all our boats were in sight, and could distinctly see the change of our direction, then he again took the lead.

Buglers were in the boat of each pilot; these sounded the "Halt," "Advance," or "Close," according to circumstances, yet, notwithstanding all this precaution and care, we lost one of the boats, with soldiers and their families in it. We halted many days for them, and, fearing they might be short of provisions, I left a boat with supplies, as soon as we entered the last clear and certain course for Calcutta, with orders to come on if the missing boat did not appear in a week. Not only is the navigation difficult and dangerous, but the low lands and banks of the channels and creeks are covered with thick mangrove-trees and scrub, and we were assured by the pilot that it was infested in many places by tigers, ever ready to pounce upon any one within their reach.

CHAPTER XXXVI

INDIA TO CAPE TOWN

The guns captured in the Sutlej campaign—Lord Hardinge's compliments to the regiment—I secure compensation for the regiment's losses at Loodhiana—Voyage to Cape Town

AT last, after more than a fortnight's exposure to the pestilential atmosphere of the mangrove marshes and swamps, and repeated causes of uncertainty and anxiety about our proper course, we arrived early in March in the Hooghly, off Fort William, and landed in safety about an hour afterwards. We were no sooner formed in line than I observed an unusual appearance—a square of artillery on the right of the direct road to the fort; and on asking an officer what that was, he told me these were all the guns captured from the enemy during the various battles on the Sutlej. I instantly determined that my brave men should enjoy a near view of these trophies and proofs of their valour, so, instead of marching direct for the fort, I made a circuitous turn toward the guns, and then all round them. The men were delighted, and their remarks were very amusing on pointing to many of the guns; for instance, "That is the fellow which knocked a whole section of ours to pieces!"; "That is the chap that knocked the colonel off his horse!"; and "Look, these are the very murdering devils which our charge settled and carried off at Aliwal!" The sight was really most gratifying, and truly calculated to inspire pride and glory in every British heart. There were in all upwards of three hundred guns of all sizes, from six to sixty-eight pounders, and principally brass, beautifully finished and mounted. After many cheers we marched into our barracks in Fort William. For the first ten days we had an increase of sick, but most of them recovered, though two or three poor men died. Our missing boat and the one left to pick it up both arrived in safety, about a fortnight after us; they were getting near the end of their provisions when they discovered their relief.

In Fort William we found the 16th Bengal Grenadiers, a regiment which wavered and held back to a man at the battle of Ferozeshah, leaving their English colonel to advance alone with our troops. He did all in his power to rally his men, but all to no purpose, so at last that brave man attached himself to our gallant 50th Regiment, and fought nobly with them, till, sad to say, he was at last killed.

Soon after our arrival at Calcutta we were asked

to dinner by the Governor-General, Lord Hardinge. He was most kind to us all, and after dinner proposed the health of "Colonel Anderson and the officers of the 50th Regiment." He made a most brilliant and flattering speech, in which he enumerated most distinctly our services in all parts of the globe, and especially spoke of our indomitable and gallant conduct in the various battles of the Sutlej; then, turning to me, he said : "You may indeed, Colonel Anderson, be proud of your noble and distinguished regiment, and I have the most sincere pleasure in drinking your health, and the health and continued success of every officer and soldier of the brave 50th."

By this time I had heard much from my officers about the extent of their losses at Loodhiana, and I determined to make a strong appeal to the Government of India for remuneration. In due course I received an answer saying it was not customary for the Government to grant any indemnity for such losses, but that I might state the nature and particulars of the losses and amount in detail, for further consideration. I communicated the answer to the officers, and requested them to furnish me with a detailed account of all their losses. When it was all complete I forwarded it to the Secretary of the Military Department, and begged that it might be favourably considered. A long time passed without my receiving an answer; but at last I got a letter informing me that the demands were unreasonable, that the officers had no claim or right to such expensive bungalows, that they should have been built in value according to their relative ranks, and that the officers' mess should not have had such costly wines. To this I replied that the comfort and health of the officers was of the first importance to the efficiency of the service, that the additional accommodation tended to their comfort and good; and with respect to the expensive and large stock of our mess wines, I said such was the custom of all officers' messes in the regiments of her Majesty's Service, and more especially in India, where the carriage was so expensive, and where the messes of British officers were expected to entertain in suitable and becoming manner, which duty they could not carry out if their supplies of wine were limited. To this I received a reply that the Government of India could not, after due consideration, grant any remuneration for the losses without establishing a precedent which must be inconvenient hereafter. I wrote once more, saying that I still ventured to make one more appeal in so just and good a cause, and stated that the officers interested were seriously inconvenienced by their losses, and by the very unexpected decision of the Government, and consequently that I considered it my imperative duty to request that the subject might be reconsidered. In another week I got an answer granting all we claimed, with the exception of a reasonable deduction from the value the officers had placed on their expensive bungalows. This then was a great victory, and my officers were indeed glad and thankful for the service I had rendered them.

Early in January, 1848, I received an order to hold the regiment in readiness for embarkation, and I was at the same time informed that one-third of the officers would be permitted to proceed home at once by the overland route, at the public expense, if they preferred it. The selection was left to me, and I was directed to forward the names at once to the Adjutant-General of her Majesty's Forces in India, that their leave of absence might appear in General Orders. Accordingly, I saw the necessity of keeping most of the senior officers to take charge of and accompany their men during the long voyage, and was happy to find that many had no particular wish to go overland. I therefore soon made my selection without disappointing any one, and amongst the number I included my own dear son. The names of the chosen few were forwarded, and in due time appeared in General Orders, with three months' leave of absence. This liberal time was given to afford them an opportunity of visiting any other parts of Europe and Asia beyond the immediate line of route. In a few days the mail steamer for Suez started, and they went off with light hearts. The arrangements and terms of the mail steamer were most liberal, for they allowed passengers to leave them at any of the ports of call for a month or six weeks, and took them up again at the same place without additional charge.

About the middle of January three splendid ships were placed at my disposal for the conveyance of my regiment to England, viz., the *Queen*, *Marlborough*, and *Sutlej*. They were all of the largest class, and, after visiting and inspecting each, I could not make up my mind which I should prefer for mine as headquarters. They were all equally tempting, and the accommodation in all most inviting and comfortable. At last I decided on the *Queen* for headquarters, and for three companies, and ordered the remainder of the regiment to be divided between the *Marlborough* and *Sutlej*, the former under the command of Captain Bonham, the latter under Major Long. In the last week in January the embarkation took place. The *Sutlej* took the lead, and the *Marlborough* followed next day, and on the morning of the 3rd February I embarked, thankful indeed to leave a land and climate which I always disliked, and with an anxious hope that I might never be doomed to visit it again.

We all were comfortable and happy on board, and our table was most amply and liberally provided. In addition to my officers we had a number of passengers, and as we had our band with us, we had music and dancing every evening. During the first three weeks the weather was very favourable, then fresh breezes and contrary winds followed occasionally, but nothing to disturb or distress us. About the middle of April we made the Cape of Good Hope, and as we approached Cape Town we were joined by, and came up with, a number of other ships, all steering for the anchorage at Table Bay. One of these in the distance appeared under three jury-masts, and to our surprise she proved to be one of our own ships, the *Sutlej*. We were now all anxiety to know the cause of her mishap and the extent of her damages and loss, fearing that some of our men must have suffered much during so serious a misfortune; but we were obliged to wait till both ships got to anchor. Then our captain and some of our officers went on board the *Sutlej*, and on their return to us reported that on the night of the 1st of April they had met a severe gale, which suddenly carried away the three masts by the deck, but fortunately without injuring any one, beyond a few bruises. They all had a most providential escape. The sea was running mountains high, and when the masts fell over the side and were being cut away clear of the hull, the end of one of them was forced through one of the dead-lights in the stern, which at once admitted the sea in tons, to a most fearful and alarming extent, and so continued for some minutes, till stopped by mattresses and some other temporary contrivances, and the pumps and dozens of buckets were kept going all the time. I was assured that even with all these precautions and means they must have foundered but for the able and willing assistance the captain and crew received from our gallant soldiers on board, for the former were all but exhausted with the previous fatigues of the gale, and the soldiers were fresh and ever ready to assist and lend a hand.

General Cartwright of the Bengal army and Major Mackay of the 21st were passengers on board, both so seriously ill that they could not leave their cabins during the disaster, and the former had a narrow escape of his life, his illness being much increased by one of the top-masts actually falling through the deck into his cabin, but fortunately clear of his bed.

CHAPTER XXXVII

RETURN TO ENGLAND

Return to England—Continued in command of the regiment

SOON after we had anchored, I landed to report our arrival, and found to my great pleasure that our old friend Sir Harry Smith commanded at the Cape. He was very glad to see us, and at once determined to land the whole of our detachment from the *Sutlej*, as the ship would require new masts and thorough repairs, which would take many weeks to carry out. They were disembarked and accommodated in barracks next morning, and on that day we all dined with Sir Harry and Lady Smith. Neither of our ships had seen our other vessel, the *Marlborough*, since the day she left us at Calcutta. We in the *Queen* remained in Table Bay for a week, and continued to receive the greatest kindness and hospitality from Sir Harry Smith. We then left and steered for St. Helena, which was reached in about ten days. We anchored there three days, and the officers were allowed to land daily if they wished. Finally we made all sail for England, without anything remarkable beyond calms and contrary winds, in consequence of which we had rather a long passage. We had no sickness on board, and our evening musical parties and dancing were continued. About the end of May we sighted the happy land of England, and on the 1st of June were off the Isle of Wight; on the morning of the 3rd we passed Deal, and there saw our good ship the *Marlborough* at anchor and without any troops on board, so we concluded at once that our detachment from that ship had landed. This was soon confirmed by a boat which boarded us and told us that they had disembarked some days before at Deal, where the depot of the regiment was stationed. Our captain continued his course according to instructions, and on the 4th of June we anchored off Gravesend; and now all was excitement and preparation for landing, and by that day's post I reported our arrival to the Adjutant-General of her Majesty's Forces at the Horse Guards. Early next day we were boarded by a staff officer from Tilbury Fort; he informed me he expected the order every minute for our landing, and requested me to prepare accordingly. We were soon all ready, and the order for our disembarkation and route for the barracks in Chatham soon came. Boats were immediately alongside, and in less than an hour the 50th Regiment was again drawn up on English ground, with the shattered but proud remains of our colours flying over us, and behind them three large new embroidered Sikh colours captured by the regiment in the battles of the Sutlej, and now the glorious trophies of our valour and renown. These, and the well-known character of the "Fighting 50th," caused great excitement and a general gathering of the inhabitants of Gravesend. There was no end to the cheering and welcomes which greeted us, and in this way the mass of the crowd followed us nearly to Chatham, and there we were received with similar honours by the commandant and all the officers and soldiers of the garrison. We dined with the officers of the garrison, and our men were feasted, and made much of by the soldiers of the different depots. Next morning we marched for Canterbury, where we halted and dined with the 21st Regiment, and went on by rail next morning to Deal, where we were met by many of our depot officers and men, and amongst the former my own dear son. We marched to our barracks and spent a very happy evening.

I had last seen my son on board the mail steamer at Calcutta, starting for England. I now learnt from him that he and his companions had stopped a few days at Cairo, and also at Alexandria, and then went on to Malta, where they remained some days. They next took their passage in a steamer for Civita Vecchia, thence by *diligence* on to Rome; they then went to Marseilles, and thence to Paris. Before they were many days in the gay capital of France, the Revolution suddenly broke out in all its horrors, and they managed by stratagem to escape from Paris, and to make their way with others to Havre, where they at once embarked for England—thankful, indeed, that they had got away with their lives, without either wounds or broken bones, considering they were for a time under fire and exposed to the risk of death. In their hurry to get away they were obliged to leave most of their clothing and baggage behind.

I was now expecting to be relieved from the command of the regiment. Colonel Woodhouse was still absent on leave, but was expected to join shortly. In another week I received an official letter informing me that I and our supernumerary lieutenants (six) would be placed on half-pay in a month from that date. This we expected, and I endeavoured to bear it in the hope of better luck, and that I might again be employed on full pay some future day—but I determined to stay with my dear regiment till Colonel Woodhouse joined. I had not to remain long, for in another week he was with us, and I, of course, handed the command over to him. Poor man, he was in bad health, and was confined to his house and could see no one. He was still commanding officer, and the adjutant carried on all details in his name. I remained packing up and preparing for my final departure, then took leave of my friends, little expecting to see them or the regiment again, and started for London.

Some days afterwards I attended the Adjutant-General's levée at the Horse Guards. He received me most kindly. After asking a few questions about the regiment and our voyage, he suddenly said, " Would you, Colonel Anderson, like to be employed again ? " My answer was ready, that most certainly I should. " Have you been with Lord Fitzroy Somerset ? " he asked (the Commander-in-Chief and Military Secretary). I replied that I had not. On which he said, " You sit here, and I will see him at once." He soon returned, and told me he could not see him then, as the Duke of Cambridge was with him, but added he would take an early opportunity of seeing Lord Fitzroy about me. Shortly after this Colonel Woodhouse retired. We all greatly regretted his loss. He had been nearly forty years in the regiment, and had commanded it for twenty-five years.

I attended Lord Fitzroy Somerset's next levée. He received me very kindly, and I mentioned my desire to be again employed. His lordship replied, " Very well, Colonel Anderson, I will make a note of it; but you had better write to me and state your wishes." He made no allusion whatever to Colonel Woodhouse, nor did I. Next day I wrote to his lordship officially, merely requesting that I might be again employed. I was some days without an answer, but I was not kept very long in suspense ere I received a letter ordering me to proceed at once to Deal, to resume the command of the 50th Regiment. This was great and glorious news, and all that my heart could desire. Next day I arrived at Deal, and was received most kindly by all. Colonel Petit handed me over the command, and I was once more at the head of my dear regiment. Colonel Petit handed me over, amongst other official papers, a letter from the Adjutant-General intimating that Colonel Woodhouse was placed on half-pay, and Lieut.-Colonel Anderson ordered to rejoin and take command of the regiment. From this time all went well, but we had all enough hard work in distributing our depot men amongst our battalion companies, preparing our new clothing, and drilling and exercising morning and evening and making everything ready for our next general inspection. About the end of July we heard of the arrival of the *Sutlej* off Gravesend, with Major Long's detachment, and in a few days they were with us. Our colonel-in-chief, General Sir George Gardner, paid us a visit about this time, and made a general inspection of the regiment. He was considered a very able and strict officer.

He now made a minute inspection, and after seeing us go through various movements, he closely inspected our interior arrangements and economy, and finally expressed himself well pleased.

CHAPTER XXXVIII

FAREWELL TO THE 50TH REGIMENT

Decide to retire—Return to Australia

I NOW heard from my wife in answer to my last letter, in which I urged her to make such arrangements for the safety and management of our property in Victoria and Melbourne as might enable her at once to return to England, and so join me. Her answer was full of good sense, saying she could not make up her mind to trust any one she knew with the entire care and management of our property; that the risk and chances of loss were too great for her to take the whole responsibility of appointing any one to act for us, and therefore, however sad our continued separation must be to us both, she considered it wise and prudent to remain where she was till she heard further from me; and I could not but concur in the wisdom of this opinion.

Having long and well considered our relative situations and the discomforts and distress which we must endure by a continued separation, I now began for the first time to think seriously about retiring from the service by the sale of my commission, and returning to my family in Australia for the rest of my life. These were serious and most trying thoughts, and not to be carried out in a hurry. To think of leaving my dear regiment for ever, and the service, to which no man was ever more devoted, and in which I had spent nearly the whole of my life, was most agonizing, and I could scarcely endure it.

At last we marched to Dover, and on the way I got into conversation with Major Petit, then the senior major of the regiment and the first for purchase. After much friendly talk I hinted to him that I would not mind retiring if I was offered a good price above the regulations. At once he asked me how much I would expect. I did not then give him any answer beyond saying I would think about it. I did think about it again and again, but I could not make up my mind, not that I hesitated about the additional sum I would ask, but about going or not going. This was towards the end of August, and I was then called on by a very dear friend, Captain Dodd, who told me he was requested by Colonel Petit and the next officers in succession for purchase to ask if I really had serious thoughts of retiring, and, if so, what additional sum I would expect. I told Captain Dodd that I had thought about it, but could not make up my mind. As I have said, he was a dear friend of mine, and we now talked long on the subject, which ended by his telling me he thought he could get them to make an additional sum of fifteen hundred pounds above the regulation. Finally I promised to make up my mind and give my final decision in a few days.

This fearful state of suspense and anxiety began to disturb my general health, and it became so bad that I could not attend parade or even leave my rooms. The surgeon attended me all this time, and recommended me to go on leave of absence, as I required a change, and it would certainly do me good. I was granted two months' sick-leave, and I promised Colonel Petit that he should have my final and positive answer in a week. In ten days' time I was really quite resigned when I saw myself gazetted out of the service, and my friend Petit and the others promoted in succession. This was a relief and great satisfaction to me, as it at once removed the anxiety I felt about them, for I sometimes doubted whether the succession and promotion would go in the regiment. A few days more brought me a letter from Colonel Petit informing me that he had instructed our agents, Messrs. Cox & Co., to place fifteen hundred pounds (beyond the regulation) to my credit, these sums making in all six thousand pounds for my commission, and so ended (on the 28th of September, 1848) my services as a soldier.

FAREWELL TO THE 50TH REGIMENT

The die was cast, the deed was done and could not be recalled, and I was indeed utterly unhappy and miserable. For forty-three years I had served my Sovereign faithfully. My whole mind and heart were devoted to my profession. I had risked my health and life in several countries and in battlefields often and often, and these memoirs show the extent of favour and success which repeatedly attended my humble endeavours. All that was now left to me was the fond remembrance of the past and the conviction that I had still, and ever would have, the heart of a soldier, and I hoped to be able to pass the remainder of my eventful life in peace and thankfulness with my dear wife and children. I must here mention such was the state of my health at this time that I had great fear that I should not live long enough to see them. But God was good and more merciful to me than I deserved; for His mercy not only restored me to them in due time, but He has granted me ever since to this day many, many of the most happy, and I may also say most healthy, years of my long life, and I am indeed thankful.

The Gresham Press,
UNWIN BROTHERS, LIMITED
WOKING AND LONDON.

www.ingramcontent.com/pod-product-compliance
Lightning Source LLC
Chambersburg PA
CBHW031134160426
43193CB00008B/137